## More Praise for *Nazarene Roots*

"This is a marvelous little book. Stan Ingersol's work sheds light on our denominational DNA through a survey of key women and men who shaped the Church of the Nazarene for over a century. Challenging, fascinating, insightful, and wise, this book sheds helpful light on the Wesleyan-Holiness movement and reminds us to continue the trajectories blazed by our forebears."

—**Jay Akkerman**, Associate Professor of Preaching and Missional Theology, Northwest Nazarene University

"Just the title of this book, *Nazarene Roots*, is an encouragement to me as a Nazarene pastor. God forbid that we would ever forget where we came from, because if we do, we won't know where we're going, and we won't know who we are when we get there."

—**Kerry W. Willis**, vision pastor, Harrisonburg, VA, First Church of the Nazarene

"Stan Ingersol is uniquely qualified and positioned to write a book such as this. His upbringing, his education, his exposure to other traditions, his life experience, his scholarship, his incredible familiarity with the historical record of the Church of the Nazarene—all these factors converge to give us this book."

—**Brad Estep**, senior pastor, Kansas City First Church of the Nazarene

"Like a sculptor, Stan Ingersol chisels through our Nazarene history to create a welcome mosaic that will be appreciated by octogenarians, 18-year-olds, and all those in between. A 'must read' and 'must own' for pastors and laity."

—**Larry Dennis**, superintendent, Central Florida District

"A historical delight for anyone who wants to deeply appreciate the theological roots and dynamic personalities of the men and women who made possible the Church of the Nazarene."

—**Stanley W. Reeder**, superintendent, Oregon Pacific District

"Every Nazarene should read Stan's new book about our holiness roots! From the founding of Providence, Rhode Island, to how the Lillenas Publishing Company became part of Nazarene Publishing House, you will find these pages filled with dozens of stories that have directly affected us all. Once you start, you won't want to put it down."

—**Larry McKain**, executive director, New Church Specialties

# A Message from Bob Broadbooks

Director, USA/Canada Office, Church of the Nazarene

Someone once said that looking at your denominational roots is like looking into a rearview mirror. If you look too long, you may bump into something ahead of you. However, if you fail to look backward, you may get hit from behind. For this reason, it is important to look into our past as we head into our future.

In 2008, we celebrated our centennial year. Since that time, we've worked to help Nazarene clergy reflect on the meaning of our 100-year journey and get better acquainted with our faith story. This has been accomplished through the Nazarene Roots Project <www.nazareneroots.org>, which is a partnership between the Nazarene Archives and the USA/Canada Office, aimed at helping pastors and church leaders better understand our faith tradition. The Nazarene Roots Project website will have materials added periodically that will not only help pastors understand their history, but also stimulate continuing holiness evangelism efforts.

Some of the resources we've developed are a CD that includes foundational documents (such as early Nazarene *Manuals*), books, articles, and a curriculum for pastors on the lessons they can learn from their faith tradition. We've also developed a DVD of a panel discussion entitled, "Reflecting on our Nazarene Heritage," which is available to clergy as a part of this effort. The panel includes Paul Bassett, Stan Ingersol, Janine Metcalf, and Tom Noble. We cover a series of topics based on questions we have received from Nazarene clergy, which include: The Church's Genesis, Founders and Shapers, Theological Vision, Major 20th Century Challenges, Holiness and Spirituality, Church Polity and Structures, The Church and Compassion, Internationalization, and Nazarene Identity (challenges and opportunities).

I would encourage you to peruse all of these materials and let us know what you think of them. We are here to support your work on the front lines of ministry, and we deeply appreciate all you do on behalf of the Church of the Nazarene and the larger body of Christ.

Pleased with the Prospects,

Bob Broadbooks

# Acknowledgements

Like every writer, I've acquired debts.

I am indebted to William McCumber, Wes Tracy, and Ev Leadingham. Each is an editor who allowed me to develop the personality-focused essays in this book. At different points in life, each has also been a friend and an inspiration.

Meri Janssen, John Bechtold, and Andrew Schwartz—colleagues in the Nazarene Archives—are a constant source of encouragement about the future. They diligently tracked down the photographs used in the book and on its cover.

Bryon McLaughlin understood this book's appropriateness as a publication related to the Nazarene Centennial. He conceptualized the layout and design, and he conceived of the various digital materials that are related to it.

Thanks, finally, to Bob Broadbooks for supporting this project with the anticipation that all who read it, especially pastors, can benefit from a renewed acquaintance with the community of saints whose lives have shaped Nazarene life and culture. Their stories are truly our own.

Nazarene Roots

# *Nazarene Roots*

*Pastors, Prophets, Revivalists & Reformers*

by

**Stan Ingersol**

ISBN: 978-0-8341-2478-3

Printed in the
United States of America

Cover Design: Arthur Cherry

Interior Layout: Tony DePina

Photo Credits: Nazarene Archives, Illustrated Bible Life (Luther Death Mask), The Library of Congress (An Older Martin Luther)

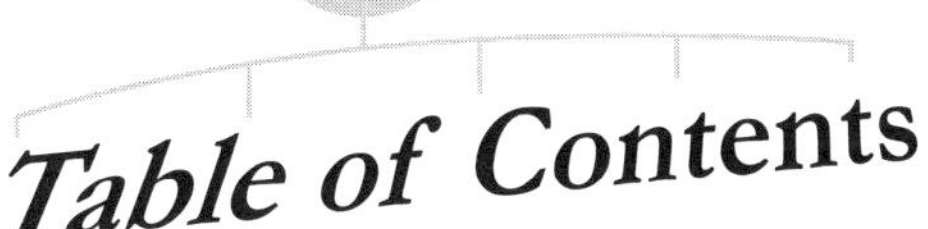

# Table of Contents

To the memory of

Timothy L. Smith

Pastor, social prophet, and historian

# Foreword

## Jesse C. Middendorf, General Superintendent

Our lives are shaped by stories which help us construct meaning, understand how to relate to our world, and build community. A story about a family ancestor has shaped my life. I'd like to share it with you.

Lewis A. Armistead was a Civil War general who faced his greatest test on the final day of the epic Battle of Gettysburg. Asked to take part in an ill-fated infantry assault later known as "Pickett's Charge," Armistead knew his men faced an insurmountable task—they knew it too—but he steadied them by waving his hat at the end of his saber as he led them into battle. Though he and many others lost their lives that day, his gesture of bravery, despite overwhelming odds, epitomized grace under fire.

Today, when I am faced with a formidable task, my resolve stiffens and my confidence in God's sustaining grace increases and I remind myself, "It's time to put your hat on the end of your sword and meet the challenge."

This story from my past provides a perspective which informs my present and future. In the same way, our denominational story renders meaning and purpose that shapes our lives. Philosopher Alasdair MacIntyre said, "I can only answer the question, 'What am I to do?,' if I can answer the prior question, 'Of what story or stories do I find myself a part?'"

"Denomination" means something very different today than it did in 1908 when our founders gathered at Pilot Point, Texas, to inaugurate the Church of the Nazarene. The optimism that genuine Christianity could speak powerfully to the issues of the day prompted some to declare the new period "the Christian Century." Early Nazarenes shared this optimism and set about the monumental task of "spreading scriptural holiness across these lands."

Now, at the beginning of a new century, we have witnessed a generation of unprecedented social and cultural change. Pluralism, secularism, and post-modernity have altered the religious landscape. Rather than a "missionary-sending country," America is itself a "mission field." Immigrants cross U.S. borders in vast numbers, people are mobile, seldom staying in one location for any length of time, and cyberspace redefines our concept of place and community.

While some may consider these developments negatively or feel a sense of drift over what it means to be Wesleyan-Holiness people, I believe our present circumstances may very well present our greatest opportunity for renewal and revitalization—as we connect with and reflect on the rich and diverse stories of our founding and shaping. Perhaps, there is no time like now to give these stories a new hearing.

In *Nazarene Roots: Pastors, Prophets, Revivalists, and Reformers*, denominational archivist Stan Ingersol brings together a series of life narratives written over a 20-year period that reveal essential truths about the people called Nazarenes. In this book, we meet some of the great heroes and heroines of the Early Church, early Methodism, and those who shaped what we know today as the "Church of the Nazarene."

Our founders were rooted in the Wesleyan-Holiness tradition. They departed established mainline churches over concerns about spiritual decline to seek broader methods to "Christianize" Christianity. They were fearless, bent on a passion to engage the neglected corners of society, and share their faith in a God whose grace could transform even the most despised.

The Church of the Nazarene started as a people movement, and we are privileged that our denominational story reflects such rich regional, cultural, and ethnic diversity. Our decision to become a truly international church is a reflection of the vision and prayers of our founders so many years ago.

Nazarene founders and shapers also had to contend with sweeping cultural change, particularly urbanization and the rise of industrial society. Rather than lose heart, they had confidence that the eternal God accompanied them along history's arc. They understood themselves to be part of a larger Christian story of God's redemptive work in the new century.

Perhaps you are encountering these stories for the first time, or you may be very familiar with the story of our Nazarene family. In either case, I think you will be challenged, stirred, and strengthened by this reflection into our past.

I pray these stories will encourage your heart, empower your ministry, and inspire you to create new chapters in the Nazarene story.

# Preface

Martin Marty once advised a group of Nazarene sociologists of religion that they and others would be well-advised to go back and study the Nazarene founders, then ask how their intentions and concerns can be translated into contemporary ministry and life. The Nazarene Roots Project takes this challenge seriously. This book is one part of that project.

There are two ways to read the intentions of founders and others who have shaped Nazarene life. One can study what they say, principally through their writings. Another approach is to study their lives. This book takes the second approach.

It is written at a popular level to be accessible for clergy and laity alike. These stories were written over a 20-year period. Most were published originally in *Herald of Holiness, World Mission, Standard,* and *Holiness Today.* They have been collected, edited, and new pieces were written to fill specific gaps. We have made this book user-friendly by omitting footnotes and other scholarly apparatus. Where documentation was needed, it appeared in the original publications and can be provided upon request. With respect to chapters 3, 4, and 5, the primary sources that were used are found in the extensive research collections of the Nazarene Archives, located in Lenexa, Kansas, where there is a collection for virtually every Nazarene written about in this book.

Stan Ingersol
Lenexa, Kansas

CHAPTER 1

# A Christian Tradition

**Introduction**

Every life is a window that opens up onto the world. This book is about Christian lives. It is about lives whose faith and witness nourished the roots of the contemporary Church of the Nazarene.

Nazarenes are relative newcomers on the scene, despite having observed a recent centennial. Paul Bassett, an esteemed professor of church history, has remarked that if all of Christian history were compressed into a single hour, the Church of the Nazarene would not appear until the last three and a half minutes. Generations of faithful disciples preceded us.

The Church of the Nazarene's "Core Values" statement affirms three values as central to this church: *Christian*, *holiness*, and *missional*. They underscore that Nazarenes are *one with the wider people of God*, Wesleyan-Holiness in *experience and theology*, and *sent into the world* as Christ was sent into it. Each affirmation bristles with implications, and each core value anchors a host of other important values.

This first chapter illuminates various dimensions of what it means to say that we are *Christian.* This affirmation may seem self-evident, but there is *context* to it that is reflected in these opening lines of the church *Manual's* "Historical Statement":

> The Church of the Nazarene, from its beginnings, has confessed itself to be a branch of the "one, holy, universal, and apostolic"

> church and has sought to be faithful to it. It confesses as its own the history of the people of God recorded in the Old and New Testaments, and that same history as it has extended from the days of the apostles to our own. As its own people, it embraces the people of God through the ages, those redeemed through Jesus Christ in whatever expression of the one church they may be found. It receives the ecumenical creeds of the first five Christian centuries as expressions of its own faith. While the Church of the Nazarene has responded to its special calling to proclaim the doctrine and experience of entire sanctification, it has taken care to retain and nurture identification with the historic church in its preaching of the Word, its administration of the sacraments, its concern to raise up and maintain a ministry that is truly apostolic in faith and practice, and its inculcating of disciplines for Christ-like living and service to others.

The essays in this chapter deal with important dimensions of Christian faith and practice. The early ones illustrate the struggles of those who contributed to the development of Christian orthodoxy—the doctrines and understandings commonly held by Christians in the Eastern Orthodox, Roman Catholic, and Protestant communities alike. Essays in the middle of the chapter touch on issues of spiritual discipline and the reform of the Christian church.

The third group of stories deal with the "religion of the heart," as Protestant pietism is often described. The Nazarenes are a people in the Pietist tradition, and for that reason it is important to know what pietism is and how it connects various strands of the Christian story. Pietism arose in the era after the Protestant Reformation, and it made inroads in various denominations throughout Europe. Methodism arose as a direct product of pietism's influence upon members of the Church of England, and Nazarenes are direct beneficiaries of this fruitful union. The stories here show that pietists have been as concerned for the poor as they have about prayer and missions, and that early Nazarene concern for the poor was not an aberration within Pietism, but a fundamental expression of its basic impulse.

## Ignatius of Antioch
### *Bishop and Martyr*

By 100, the Christian churches were home to a variety of theologies. Some were compatible with one another, while others were not. Some forms of Christianity were still tied to Judaism; distinctly Gentile forms of Christianity held sway in other quarters.

> "As God's athlete, be sober; the stake is immortality and eternal life."

Christian writings circulated, but the New Testament as a defined body of scriptures would not exist for another 100 years. Churches in Asia Minor highly regarded the writings of Paul. The Syrians promoted the Gospel of Matthew. The Alexandrians, in Egypt, treasured yet other Christian writings. The Hebrew Bible (Old Testament) was the only text that all Christians accepted as sacred scriptures.

Ignatius was the Christian bishop in Antioch at this time. He succeeded Euodius, who in turn succeeded St. Peter. The date when Ignatius became bishop is unknown, but he died, probably as a martyr, between 107 and 117, during the persecutions of the Roman emperor Trajan.

> "Please pray for me . . . that I may not only speak the truth but become the truth; that I may not only be called a Christian, but also live like a Christian."

Ignatius led one of the most important Christian communities of his day. Antioch had been the first important Christian center outside Jerusalem. The city ranked with Alexandria as a Roman center for the eastern Mediterranean. Christianity was planted among Antioch's large Jewish population in the late 30s, then spread to the city's Gentile population.

Barnabas, Paul, and Peter had important ministries here. Paul and Peter clashed here over whether Gentile Christians must also convert to Judaism. From Antioch the Christian mission to Asia Minor and Cyprus was planned as Paul and Barnabas, later joined by Silas and John Mark, were sent as missionaries. Here the disciples "were first called Christians" (Acts 11:26)—an indication that in Antioch they were perceived as distinct from Jews at an early date. There is evidence that Matthew's Gospel was written in Antioch, and even stronger evidence that it was disseminated from this early Christian center. Ignatius led a church, then, with double apostolic foundations.

His seven letters to various churches in Asia Minor reflect the development of Antiochene Christianity. By Ignatius' day, the church in Antioch had a three-fold ministry: the *episkopos* (bishop or overseer), the *presbuteroi* (elders), and the *diakonoi* (deacons or servants). This structure of ministry was spurred by more than simple evolution—his letters reflect Ignatius' concern over newly emergent heresies about Christ's nature that threatened the church's doctrine of salvation. Ignatius believed the bishop to be a protector of sound doctrine and a focus of unity. The linkage was critical: heresy was not a mere difference of religious opinion; it tended to disintegrate Christian communities.

Ignatius contended especially against the heresy of Docetism, which denied Christ's essential humanity. Docetic Christians worshiped Christ as divine and regarded him as a spirit-being who was never really enfleshed, who never actually tasted human life, suffering, or death in the full and actual sense. Docetists believed that Jesus appeared to live in the flesh without actually doing so.

"He who died in place of us is the one object of my quest. He who rose for our sakes is my one desire."

Against this view, Ignatius asserted the full humanity and divinity of Christ. He emphasized Jesus' lineage from David and asserted that he was truly born of a woman, truly ate and drank, truly suffered and died, was truly resurrected physically, and truly lives in resurrected flesh today. At the same time, Ignatius clearly asserted that Jesus is God—that he was both "begotten and unbegotten," "both from Mary and from God."

The Eucharist (Holy Communion) was important to Ignatius. By letter, he urged the Christians of Ephesus to "be eager for more frequent gatherings for [Eucharistic] thanksgiving to God. . . . For when you meet frequently the forces of Satan are annulled and his destructive power is cancelled."

At some point in Trajan's reign (98-117), Ignatius was arrested and sent to Rome. His seven letters to churches in Asia Minor were written on this journey. They show his vivid expectation of martyrdom. He was allowed to meet with Christian groups along the route, and at Smyrna, near the Aegean coast, he talked with that city's bishop, Polycarp, who would be martyred around 155.

The testimony of St. Ignatius symbolizes the Early Church's struggle against enemies within and without.

### Athanasius
### *Bishop of Alexandria*

Early Christianity was an urban religion that spread from Jerusalem to other Mediterranean cities. St. Paul's epistles—addressed to Christians in Ephesus, Philippi, Corinth, Thessalonica, and Rome—underscore the Early Church's urban character. Christian missionaries went initially to cities with large Jewish populations, and more Jews lived in Alexandria, Egypt, than in Jerusalem.

Alexandria was founded by Alexander the Great in Egypt around 330 B.C. The city boasted the Pharos, a spectacular lighthouse that was one of the Seven Wonders of the Ancient World, and a great library that had no peer.

Athanasius

By 319, Christian churches were scattered throughout Alexandria. They were united under the leadership of Bishop Alexander, whose secretary and protégé, Athanasius, was a native of the city and possessed a strong theological bent.

In that year, Arius, the popular pastor of one of the suburban churches, began preaching that Christ was neither truly God nor truly human, but a person of an intermediate order. Arius taught that God had created Christ before the world; in turn, Christ had created the universe. Arius believed his views were grounded in scriptures that stressed the Son of God's subordination to the Father. He further justified his interpretations by appealing to the writings of theologians he believed substantiated his views.

Arius was deposed from his parish in 321, but his ideas did not disappear. He spread his views in other countries and won the backing of Eusebius of Nicomedia, an influential bishop who had the ear of the Roman emperor Constantine. In 325, Constantine called the First Ecumenical Council to address the issues involved in the Arian controversy. Athanasius attended the council as Bishop Alexander's assistant.

"What the soul does in all the members of one body, this the Holy Spirit does throughout the Church."

The Council of Nicea largely represented the churches of the Eastern Mediterranean, or the Greek-speaking sector of Christendom. The Latin-speaking churches to the West were not as well represented. The Arian position had strong support, and the Arians argued that the Father and Son were "of a similar substance." But the Council concluded that the Father and the Son were *homoousian*—"of the same substance." Thus the essential unity of the First and Second Persons of the Godhead was affirmed.

Athanasius succeeded Alexander as bishop three years later. He was only 32 years old. The Arian party did not see the Council's decision as final and continued to press its case wherever it found a hearing. Over the next 40 years, Athanasius was the principal champion of Nicene theology and the principal opponent of the Arians.

The Arian party drew strength by allying itself to imperial power. Indeed, Constantine was baptized shortly before his death by the Arian bishop, Eusebius of Nicomedia. It was Eusebius who persuaded Constantine that Arius should be reinstated as a priest in Alexandria.

When Athanasius refused the emperor's request, Constantine deposed and sent him into exile in 335. This was the first of several exiles Athanasius endured as his fortunes rose and fell with political tides.

He was reinstated upon Constantine's death in 338, but two years later, the emperor of the Eastern Roman Empire, Constantius, sent him into exile again. Athanasius spent this second exile in Rome. He was welcomed by the bishop and leaders in this bastion of orthodoxy and was honored by Constans, emperor of the Western Roman Empire. A synod of Latin bishops meeting in Rome in 340 (or 341) upheld the Nicene faith and supported Athanasius. The two emperors also called a joint council that met in 343. The Arian party was outnumbered and withdrew, and the council vindicated Athanasius and his doctrine of the Godhead.

Armed by this victory, Athanasius returned to Alexandria in 346 and resumed his episcopal office. His troubles were not over. In 353, Constans died, and the Arian sympathizer Constantius consolidated his rule over both halves of the empire. Athanasius and other Eastern bishops who supported Nicene theology were exiled in 356. This time, Athanasius stayed with Egyptian monks in the desert. He returned after Constantius' death in 361.

He was exiled and restored twice more before his death in 373. His persistent advocacy of the Nicene theology built support for this view among priests and bishops through the Eastern Church and laid the groundwork for its triumph in the Council of Constantinople in 381. For this reason, Athanasius is remembered as a shaper of Christian orthodoxy and a defender of the faith.

## Augustine
### *North African Saint*

Modern Christians tend to think of North Africa as a mosaic of Islamic nations, often forgetting that Christianity once had strong centers there. The conversion of one North African in 386 proved to be an event that altered Christian history. St. Augustine, as he was later declared, was an intellectual whose journey to the Christian faith has enduring value.

Augustine was born in 354 in Tagaste (in present-day Algeria), near the Phoenician city of Carthage, which once vied with Rome for dominance of the Mediterranean. Rome's victory over Carthage in the

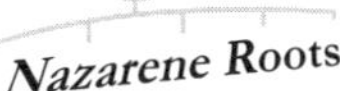


second century B.C. brought that sector of North Africa under Roman rule and helped start the process of a Roman empire.

By Augustine's birth 500 years later, North Africa was thoroughly Latin in culture and religion. Augustine's parents followed different religions. Monica was a Christian, while Patricius, a Roman official, was a pagan. Augustine's mind was eager and bright. Patricius made sure that his son attended the best schools, and Augustine mastered the curriculum of the day, grounded in Greek and Roman literature. He was attracted especially to rhetoric, and the Roman philosopher Cicero was an important influence on Augustine's thinking.

Augustine

His god was that of the philosophers, not the God of Christian faith. In his late teens, he took, in pagan fashion, a concubine who bore a son, Adeodatus ("gift from God"). He was a successful teacher of rhetoric in Carthage, and in 383, they moved to Italy, where Augustine taught first in Rome and then in Milan. He hoped to marry into a well-connected family and secure a good position in government.

"You have made us for yourself, O Lord, and our hearts are restless until they rest in you."

Monica had long sought her son's conversion to Christ, but Augustine regarded her religion as intellectually unworthy. For some years, he adhered to Manichaeanism, a Gnostic religion that shared Augustine's dislike of the Old Testament and saw the world in terms of a conflict between divine spirit and sinful matter. But in Milan, Augustine came under the influence of the great preacher-bishop Ambrose, whose sermons set forth a Christian philosophy sturdy enough to match Augustine's roving intellect. Monica joined her son in Milan and persuaded Augustine to put his concubine away. In 386, he and Adeodatus converted to Christianity and were baptized on Easter 387 by Ambrose. Monica died later that year.

In 390, Augustine and his son returned to North Africa and started a community of Christian philosophers at Tagaste. But Adeodatus died a short time later. The loneliness of losing so many close relatives pushed Augustine toward a total dedication of his life to Christian service. He was ordained a priest the following year at Hippo, a city east of Carthage, and five years later, he became its bishop, an office he held for 34 years.

Augustine

There were hundreds of bishops in the Roman empire. Augustine was distinguished from the rest by the breadth of his sanctified intellect. Apart from the routine work of church administration and preaching, he wrote voluminously. The most significant works were his *Confessions* (400), *The City of God* (426), and a major treatise on the Trinity.

"God has no need of your money, but the poor have. You give it to the poor, and God receives it."

Augustine's *Confessions* was an autobiography laced with theological reflection. Its opening paragraph, framed as a prayer to God, contains one of the most famous lines in Christian history: "You have made us for yourself, and our hearts are restless until they find their rest in you."

The plunder of Rome by the Goths in 410 prompted Augustine to write *The City of God*. Pagans argued that Rome's humiliation occurred because the old deities had been abandoned by Christians. Augustine answered, setting forth a Christian philosophy of history. He argued that there have been two cities since Adam's fall—the earthly city and the heavenly one. In a sense, they are parallel lines of history. The heavenly city is what counts. The decline of an empire is not important in the larger scheme of God's intentions.

Augustine

In 429, marauding Vandals passed through Spain and crossed the sea to North Africa, turning east toward Carthage. Refugees streamed out of the cities in their path. Augustine sent some priests with the refugees. These were to return and restore the church after the Vandals moved on. He and other priests stayed with the city's defenders. By mid-430, Hippo was besieged, but Augustine did not see it fall to the Vandals. In the midst of the siege, he fell sick and died.

His writings became important theological resources for the church. Medieval Catholics leaned on Augustine's doctrine of the church, while Protestant reformers of the 16th century relied on Augustine's understanding of sin and redemption.

### Catherine of Siena
#### *Mystic and Theologian*

The religious pulse of the Middle Ages is best taken in the various spiritual renewal movements and in the scores of monasteries and convents where holiness was generally, if not always, pursued. Women were vital contributors to medieval piety. John Wesley referred to some of them as relevant examples of devotion to God, as did his heirs in the 19th-century Holiness Movement. Among the notable women who shaped medieval piety were Julian of Norwich, Hildegard of Bingen, Bridget of Sweden, Catherine of Genoa, Teresa of Avila, and Catherine of Siena.

"Charity is the sweet and holy bond which links the soul with its Creator."

A medieval woman pursuing a life devoted solely to God sometimes chose to be a hermitess, where her life of prayer was lived in lonely isolation from all other fellowship but God's. Women were more likely to

become nuns, living in community with spiritual sisters.

But there was also a third option — that of tertiary.

A tertiary was a layperson aligned with the goals and spiritual exercises of a monastic order, but who lived out in the world, not in isolation or behind a convent wall. There were male and female tertiaries, married and single ones. Tertiaries brought the pursuit of holiness out of the monasteries and convents into ordinary homes. Perhaps the most impressive medieval tertiary was a woman—Catherine of Siena.

"O eternal Trinity,
You are a deep sea in
which the more I seek, the more I find;
and the more I find,
the more I seek
to know You."

Catherine was born into a large family in Siena, Italy, in 1347. She was the 24th of 25 children. At six, she experienced a vision of Jesus that changed her life. The next year, she privately vowed to remain a lifelong virgin. She objected strongly when her parents tried to arrange a marriage for her a few years later. Finally, they accepted her viewpoint and provided her a room where she could live a life of prayer, meditation, and solitude. In this life of piety and religious exercises, she ate her meals alone and withdrew from the family's social life, leaving her room only to attend church. This was Catherine's pattern for six years. During this period, she was accepted by the Dominican order as a tertiary.

Catherine of Siena

At 21, Catherine experienced a vision that again reoriented her life. She felt divinely led to rejoin the table and hearth fellowship of her family, and to re-engage the world. The other female tertiaries in Siena were active in caring for the sick and poor of the city. Catherine joined them in this work, and the hospitals and homes of the sick became her place of ministry.

Catherine's buoyant faith inspired others, not only those in her care but also priests and theologians, who were impressed by the quality of her spiritual life and theological curiosity. Able to read but not write, she learned serious theology by dialoguing with priests and other churchmen. They, in turn, recognized her leadership in spiritual living.

In time, Catherine attracted a cadre of followers who looked to her example and took her advice on spiritual matters.

She was active in settling many local disputes. As her reputation spread beyond Siena, she found herself, in 1374, trying to negotiate peace between the city of Florence and the church. The deception of the Florentines nullified her efforts, but her reputation as a peacemaker was not hurt. When the bubonic plague swept through Siena later that year, Catherine tended the sick and dying with a reckless abandon, caring little for her own life and welfare. Her confidence was always in God's providence and care.

Catherine dictated scores of letters. Her correspondents included popes, princes, leaders of various cities and states, and ordinary people seeking advice. She learned to write when she was nearly 30 and used this new skill to write several treatises on the devotional life. Her major work was *The Dialogue*, a lengthy book of over 340 pages in its recent English-language translation. *The Dialogue* reflects Catherine's mystical theology and her concern for the "way of perfection."

By her early 30s, Catherine was involved in the greatest crisis facing the church of her day. The Catholic Church faced a scandalous situation where there were two rival popes. Catherine wanted to see the church healed and labored hard to bring about that healing. At the same time, she supported one of the rival popes enthusiastically. Her involvement took her to Rome, where she died at age 33.

Catherine of Siena's spiritual theology—derived in large degree not from church doctrines, but her own experience of God and her meditations on the nature of God's trinity, incarnation, and grace—was so influential that she is one of two women recognized by her church today as a "doctor," or theologian, of the church.

**John Huss**
***Prophet and Martyr***

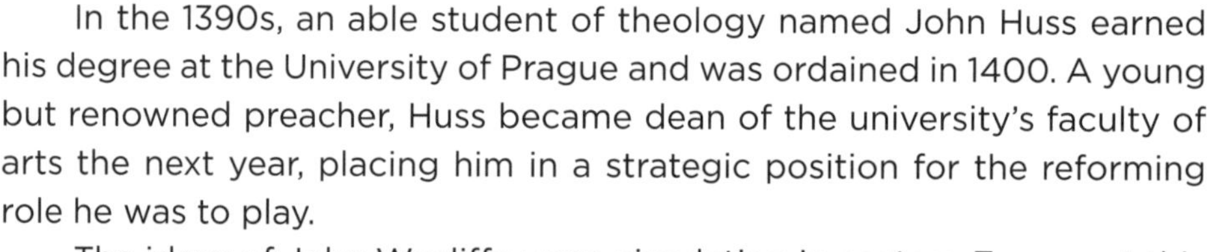

In the 1390s, an able student of theology named John Huss earned his degree at the University of Prague and was ordained in 1400. A young but renowned preacher, Huss became dean of the university's faculty of arts the next year, placing him in a strategic position for the reforming role he was to play.

John Huss

The ideas of John Wycliffe were circulating in eastern Europe at this time. Wycliffe had set forth ideas for the reform of the Roman Catholic Church while teaching at Oxford University. After his death in 1381, these ideas were spread in England by traveling preachers, called Lollards, and throughout Europe by theology students and sympathetic scholars. Wycliffe emphasized the primacy of Scripture and the importance of preaching as a greater means of grace than the sacraments. He also believed that clergy should be poor for the gospel's sake and asked the state to confiscate church lands so that the clergy would be less preoccupied with secular affairs and fix their attention on spiritual matters.

These ideas found fertile soil in the Czech state of Bohemia and its capital, Prague. Bohemia was Catholic but had a degree of independence from Rome. This was partly due to Bohemia's prosperity, and partly because its church was aligned with Eastern Orthodoxy until the 1300s. Thus, Czech ties to Rome were not ancient, and upon aligning with the Western church, the Bohemians negotiated a degree of independence, continuing to follow certain customs common to the Orthodox Church but not the Catholic one. When Wycliffe's ideas reached Prague, they were thrown into this devout but independent-minded religious environment.

The University of Prague served not only Bohemia, but Poland and the German states of Saxony and Bavaria. The German students were less sympathetic than the Czechs to Wycliffe's ideas, and in 1403, they presented a document with 45 points drawn from Wycliffe's writings that they wanted the university to condemn. The reform party chose Huss to defend Wycliffe's writings in the ensuing debate. As he prepared for the debate, Huss read Wycliffe thoroughly and became an able expositor of his ideas.

In the years that followed, Huss rose in favor. He became a court chaplain and a confessor of the Queen. He used his position at the university and in Czech national life to advocate the reform of Catholicism.

By 1409, Huss was at odds with the archbishop of Prague. In one of medieval history's quirkiest moments, the Roman Catholic Church was in the odd situation of having two rival popes, each one duly elected, and much of western Europe divided by the question of which was the legitimate leader of the church. In Bohemia, Archbishop Zbynek favored one of the contenders, but Huss and others at the university believed that both claimants should be deposed by a church council and replaced by a leader who could unify the church. So, too, did the Bohemian king, Wentzel. And the Council of Pisa eventually did just that. Huss, meanwhile, was promoted to rector of the university. Thereafter, he and the archbishop were at odds with one another.

Their next confrontation came over Wycliffe's writings, which Archbishop Zbynek tried to suppress and publicly burned. Huss and the university's theology faculty dissented strongly and publicly, and were excommunicated for their defiant stance against church authority. But King Wentzel struck a deal with the new pope, and Huss' excommunication was lifted. He continued developing his theology of reform based on Wycliffe's doctrines.

Execution of John Huss

In 1412, Huss began attacking the practice of papal indulgences—the idea that sin could be absolved by the pope or his agents. The pope had declared a crusade against an Italian opponent and promised indulgences to those fighting for his cause or sending money to aid it. Huss, however, argued that God alone can forgive sins, and insisted that church leaders use spiritual weapons, not the same weapons as secular rulers. He advised Czech Christians to turn a deaf ear to the pope's appeal.

The pope ordered Huss' seizure and excommunication, but Huss went into hiding and continued writing. His views were popular with the people of his homeland.

In 1414, the Council of Constance met, partly to settle the Bohemian crisis. Huss was invited to attend and promised safe-conduct. He decided to go make his case in person, but upon arriving, he was arrested, later tried for heresy, and sentenced to death. Huss was burned at the stake in July 1415.

His execution provoked a bloody civil war in Bohemia and drove a deeper wedge than before between the national church and Rome. After a long period of social instability, a Hussite archbishop, John Rokycana, was installed in Prague, and the Bohemian church negotiated a still larger degree of national freedom, including the election of church officials in Bohemia by clergy and laity.

Huss and the Czech national church proved to be a bellwether of the coming Reformation.

### Martin Luther
### *Prophet of the Word*

Roman Catholicism determined western Europe's religious orientation for over a millennium, but this ended with Martin Luther. Movements to reform spiritual life in the Middle Ages were successfully incorporated

within the church, but those seeking doctrinal reform met resistance and were pushed into sectarian dissent. Luther's reform of church doctrine fared differently, and Lutheranism became an international force that altered the state church in several nations and opened the door to other forms of Protestantism, including Calvinism and Anabaptism.

Martin Luther as an Augustinian Friar, age 37, by Lucas Cranach, 1520

Martin Luther was born in Eisleben, in the German state of Saxony, in 1483. He was baptized on the day honoring St. Martin of Tours and received that saint's name. Raised in Mansfield, he attended its Latin school, and later the cathedral school at Magdeburg. In 1501, he entered the University of Erfurt, completed his Master's degree, and began studying law. But in 1505, he suddenly dropped out and sought admission in the local Augustinian monastery. Against his father's wishes, Luther took monastic vows in 1506. He was ordained a priest the next year.

Luther's fine mind led to an appointment to teach ethics at the University of Wittenberg. A colleague, Johann Staupitz, taught Biblical Theology. Luther took a degree in Bible from Staupitz, who arranged for Luther to succeed him in 1512.

"The Bible is the cradle wherein Christ is laid."

Luther had grown to disdain philosophy and love biblical study. He was also a disciple of St. Augustine's theology, an antidote to the philosophical and speculative theology of Luther's day. Augustine's search for truth resonated with Luther's own spiritual restlessness and uncertainty of salvation.

Staupitz, his confessor, said that Luther suffered "scruples"—an overweening sense of guilt without objective basis. Luther was not consoled. His salvation seemed hostage to a legalistic system of merit that overwhelmed him. When he read in Scripture of God's "justice," Luther saw himself as one under sentence of death.

Philip Melanchthon, Luther's Right Hand Man

The breakthrough came one day when he realized that the "justice of God" is not God's divine wrath, but a sentence of forgiveness and freedom in Christ. Armed with this insight, Luther rethought his whole theology, breaking through to a new understanding of the gospel based on salvation by grace through faith.

Soon after, Luther came into conflict with John Tetzel, a monk commissioned by the pope to sell indulgences. Penance had three parts: a contrite heart, confession, and satisfaction (a restitutionary act). The indulgence only affected the last part—the act by which one gives a sign of their sorrow over sin. But Tetzel's indulgence promised full remission of sins. Luther was aghast! Did the poor and ignorant understand that true repentance involved contrition, or did they think they could purchase a

"Every man must do two things alone; he must do his own believing and his own dying."

An Older Martin Luther

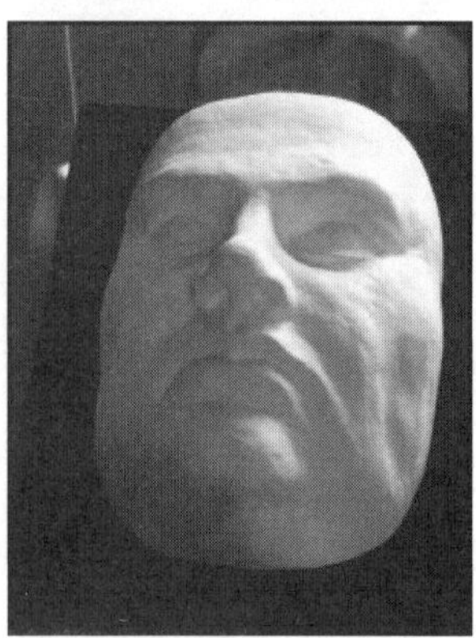
Luther Death Mask

license to sin? Luther believed that many regarded Tetzel's indulgences in the latter light and were being led astray.

He drew up 95 points, or theses, challenging the doctrine of penance and posted it, seeking a public debate. There were no takers. But someone had them printed, and they spread quickly throughout Germany. Wittenberg became the center of a breaking storm.

Luther revised the theology curriculum at Wittenberg, grounding it in biblical studies. He advocated a "Theology of the Cross" in opposition to what he termed Catholicism's contemporary "Theology of Glory." He questioned the church's use of excommunication for trivial purposes and was subjected to an investigation by Cardinal Cajetan. A series of writings in 1520 set forth a new understanding of the sacraments that undercut Roman Catholic notions, argued for limiting papal influence, supported clergy marriage, and recommended that the church in Germany be placed solely under a German bishop.

In 1521, Luther was excommunicated and his arrest sought, but he was protected by his prince, who secured him a hearing before Emperor Charles V and the German Diet. Luther's defense of his theology gained him support among certain princes, but not the Emperor, who ordered his arrest. It was never carried out. Luther hid for awhile and then returned to Wittenberg, where Prince Frederick and his successor protected him, allowing him to teach until his death.

His accomplishments were considerable: A translation of the New Testament in German based on a restored Greek text, a new order of worship for the Lutheran churches, and theological writings so voluminous that they fill entire shelves. By Luther's death in 1546, the Reformation of Western Christianity had taken a firm hold in Northern Europe and the map of the Christian world had been redrawn.

**Thomas Cranmer**
***Father of the English Reformation***

There was no death-bed for Thomas Cranmer. Instead, he was tied to the stake at Oxford and burned to death.

A common stereotype holds that the Reformation on continental Europe was driven by theological issues, while the English Reformation sprang from Henry VIII's desire for a divorce. While the divorce issue created a fissure between the English monarch and the papacy, the fissure

was widened by a growing desire to reform church doctrine and worship, as Cranmer's life and work demonstrates.

Thomas Cranmer

Thomas Cranmer was born in 1489 and sent to Cambridge University at age 22. He married in 1515, but his wife died in childbirth, so he returned to the university, studied theology, and was ordained as a Roman Catholic priest in 1520. He taught at Cambridge for a decade, leaving when Henry VIII appointed him to be the English ambassador to the court of Charles V, Emperor of the Holy Roman Empire.

Cranmer's years in Germany introduced him firsthand to Lutherans and their influence, and he gravitated increasingly toward Protestant thinking. In a few short years, Cranmer's sympathies were more Lutheran than Catholic. There is more: marriage was forbidden to priests, but in Germany Cranmer secretly took a Lutheran bride who was the niece of Andreas Osiander, a Protestant theologian and reformer.

In Europe, he learned that he was to become Archbishop of Canterbury. He returned to England and was formally consecrated to the office in 1533.

> "If there were any word of God beside the Scripture, we could never be certain of God's Word; and if we be uncertain of God's Word, the devil might bring in among us a new word, a new doctrine, a new faith, a new church, a new god, yea himself to be a god."

Cranmer was plunged into Henry VIII's struggle to separate the English Church from the papacy. The monasteries were closed, and an act of Parliament formally announced the separation of the English church from the pope. Another law made the king the "supreme head" of the Church of England. Most of the early reforms were driven by Henry, who had some theological acumen and a strategy for re-writing the relationship between the English church and wider Christendom. Nevertheless, Henry leaned in the Roman direction on several theological issues, including the Eucharistic doctrine of transubstantiation and the celibacy of priests, which were reaffirmed in decrees of 1539, leading Cranmer to send his wife back to Germany.

In time, Cranmer emerged as the more significant figure in the theological and liturgical reform of the Church of England. Henry cannily put Protestants in charge of educating the crown prince Edward, and the boy ascended to the throne when Henry died in 1547. Cranmer moved more decisively after Henry's death. Images were removed from churches, and England opened its borders to Protestant refugees from Europe. Cranmer's primary contributions, however, came in three important areas.

First, he was the primary author of *The Prayer Book of 1549*. *The Prayer Book* was a manual for public and private worship. Cranmer reduced the number of daily services to two, and he wrote it in a broad manner to appeal to those of different persuasions. His wanted to unite

Thomas Cranmer

England around worship. *The Prayer Book* was published in English, not Latin, and emphasized Bible readings in the worship services. In 1552, it was revised to remove lingering vestiges of the Latin mass.

Second, Cranmer was the primary writer of the 42 Articles of Religion, a doctrinal statement for the Church of England. It was Protestant to the core. While it reflected Lutheran influences, it also shows that Cranmer's reading in Protestant sources had shifted his perspective toward Zwingli and Calvin.

His third influence was exerted through the *Book of Homilies,* containing model sermons that set forth the fundamental themes of Protestant thought. Cranmer wrote most of its sermons. The homilies were to be read publicly in the churches since many local priests were ignorant of the new theology or resistant to it. They were designed to promote sound doctrine.

Edward VI died after six years on the throne. He was succeeded by his oldest sister, Mary, a staunch Roman Catholic, who sought to restore the Roman Catholic Church in England. Cranmer and other Protestant leaders were imprisoned. He was convicted of treason in 1553, then sent to Oxford to be tried for heresy. His heresy trial occurred simultaneously with the trials of reforming bishops Nicholas Ridley and Hugh Latimer, who were burned back-to-back at Oxford on October 16, 1555. Cranmer was forced to watch their excruciating deaths from a nearby window.

Cranmer's execution depicted in *Foxe's Book of Martyrs*

His courage and resolve wavered in the days ahead. Under pressure to recant Protestant teachings, he finally did so in writing. Yet, given an opportunity to recant publicly before a crowd at University Church, he surprised his jailers by disavowing his recantations and reaffirming his Protestant beliefs. He was taken immediately and burned. As the flames gathered round him, Cranmer took his writing hand, with which he had signed the recantations, and plunged it into the flames to burn first. He died on March 21, 1556.

Mary's reign lasted only until 1558, when she died of an illness. Her sister, Elizabeth I, ascended to the throne and moved England back into the Protestant camp. Cranmer's doctrinal statement was revised and

reissued as the 39 Articles of Religion of the Church of England. And the *Book of Common Prayer* was restored to the place of use and honor that Cranmer had intended it to have.

**Roger Williams**
***Separating Church and State***

The Church of England contained three contending parties when New England's Plymouth Colony was planted in 1621. Episcopalians supported the ancient system of bishops; Presbyterians wanted bishops replaced with governing councils called presbyteries; and Independents wanted the Church of England to become congregational in government, without bishops or presbyteries. Both Presbyterians and Independents were Puritans.

> "That cannot be a true religion which needs carnal weapons to uphold it."

But their leaders were persecuted, and many Independents doubted that the state church would ever accept their vision, so many sailed to the New World and established a purified church in the American wilderness. They were not *separatists,* as often portrayed, but regarded themselves as a reformed branch of the Church of England. Nothing put this more clearly in focus than the arrival in Boston of a *real* separatist, Roger Williams.

> "Enforced uniformity confounds civil and religious liberty and denies the principles of Christianity and civility. No man shall be required to worship or maintain a worship against his will."

Williams was born about 1603. Sir Edward Coke, a famed jurist, extended his patronage to young Williams, enabling the boy to attend Charterhouse School in London—the same school John Wesley attended a century later. Williams proceeded to college at Cambridge, receiving his degree in 1627. He became a chaplain to a wealthy household and, in 1629, married one of the maids, Mary Barnard.

Williams was identified firmly with the Puritan party in the Church of England by this time, and in 1630, he and Mary sailed for New England, arriving in Massachusetts in early 1631. Williams was offered a position as teacher in Boston's church, but he refused it, for he had come to reject the idea of a state church in principle—whether Episcopal or Puritan in form.

He accepted a similar position in Plymouth, but his two years there were controversial. He tried to persuade his fellow colonists to break off completely from the Church of England—in theory as well as in fact—and he advocated strict separation of church and state. He argued, especially, that civil officials had no business enforcing the first four commandments. These commandments were to be obeyed voluntarily; God is not truly served through worship that is coerced. These views were controversial. In 1633, Williams accepted an offer to pastor Salem's congregation, but he was marked as a dissenter by other Massachusetts leaders. In October 1635, he was banished from the colony. To avoid deportation, he fled into the wilderness and lived with Indians he had befriended while at Plymouth.

The following summer, he purchased land from the Indians and, with help from friends, started a settlement later named Providence. In 1638, they worked out a government. Their covenant made no mention of religion; the covenant strictly governed civil life and nothing else. Williams later commented that he wanted Providence to be a "shelter for persons distressed for conscience." And so it became. Baptists, Quakers, Jews, and Roman Catholics flocked to the Rhode Island colony. So did refugees from Massachusetts, including Anne Hutchinson.

Throughout his life, Roger Williams was vexed by the issue of the visible church. How should the true church be constructed? He rejected the Episcopal forms of the church of his youth, and the Presbyterian and Congregational forms of Puritanism as well. In 1639, he welcomed to Providence a group of Baptists led by John Clarke. Under their influence, he was rebaptized and joined in establishing the first Baptist congregation in America. But in a short while, he was disillusioned and withdrew from the congregation. He adopted a new religious stance that he maintained thereafter—that of a Seeker. As a Seeker, he looked forward to the Holy Spirit's action to reestablish apostolic Christianity. In the meantime, he judged all the existing churches to be less than apostolic.

Williams was vigilant in defense of Rhode Island's religious liberty throughout his days. He returned to England in 1643, seeking a charter from the English government to legalize the Rhode Island colony and guarantee its status. This was granted in 1644. While in London, Williams published *The Bloudy Tenet of Persecution*, arguing that none should be persecuted on account of their conscience. "True civility and Christianity may both flourish in a state or Kingdome" that allows people of diverse consciences to live. The blood of so many Catholics and Protestants killed in religious wars "is not required or accepted by Jesus Christ the Prince of Peace." And he insisted that ancient Israel was unique in its covenant relationship with God, and not intended by God as a model for His relationship with other nations. After Christ's coming, Williams argued, Israel was only a model for the church, not the state.

Roger Williams died in 1683. His legacy lay in his contribution to modern doctrines of religious liberty. Under his leadership, Rhode Island was the first modern state that made religious liberty a cornerstone of citizenship.

### Philip Jacob Spener
### *German Pietist*

Early Methodism was described as the "religion of the warmed heart." The phrase is rooted in John Wesley's experience at Aldersgate Street—a moment of deep realization of divine grace, of which he said: "My heart was strangely warmed."

Philip Jacob Spener

"The Word of God remains the seed from which all that is good in us must grow."

Wesley aptly described the chief concern of *pietism*, a European Protestant movement that altered the character of world Christianity. Pietism's themes are familiar to Wesleyan-Holiness people: conviction of sin and conversion to God, justification by faith as a "lived" experience, the witness of the Spirit, and holy living by the power of divine grace. Methodists, the pietistic vanguard in the Church of England, were heirs of an impulse older than they. They were among the many heirs of Philip Jacob Spener.

Spener was born into a Lutheran household near Strasbourg, in the Alsace region of Germany, in 1635. His father was the steward of a local duke. Spener was a religious youth, a trait of his mother's influence. He entered Strasbourg's university at 16 and, after receiving a degree, remained to teach history and study theology. Then he traveled for several years. In Geneva, he was attracted to the preaching of the noted French Calvinist, Jean de Labadie, whose devotional bent influenced Spener.

He returned to Strasbourg and earned a doctorate in theology. Marriage and ordination to the Lutheran ministry followed. In 1666, he became the senior minister in Frankfurt am Main, active in the ministry of Frankfurt's central church and supervisor of the city's 12 other clergy.

Spener emphasized the laity's role in the church's spiritual life. In 1670, he formed what he called *collegia pietatis*, or holy fellowships. In these small groups, lay people held one another accountable for their discipleship. Spener saw these groups as central for renewing Lutheranism and other Protestant churches.

The theologies of the Reformation had settled into new orthodoxies maintained by the power of European state churches. Spener understood that it was possible to know everything about Jesus Christ and yet know nothing of him. One could be a practicing Lutheran or Calvinist with no actual experience of divine grace. This was true for theologians and common laborers alike. The Reformation doctrines needed to be carried deeper, until they were living realities in the lives of ordinary people.

Spener set forth his program for religious reform in a book, *Pia Desideria*. Its six points included a new emphasis on the Word of God through preaching and Bible study, an understanding of lay people as priests and ministers before God, and the awareness that true faith is rooted more in steady practice than adherence to orthodoxy.

August Hermann Francke

Spener's fourth point was that Christians should beware of their conduct in controversies with unbelievers and heretics. Christians should show heartfelt love toward infidels and heretics, since love—not disputing—is the way God's truth is made known to others. Spener's final proposals concerned the ordained ministry: clergy should be true Christians in heart and life and not merely orthodox and conservative in their opinions, and the goal of preaching should be to breed faith and the fruits of the Spirit in the people.

The small-group movement grew in spite of resistance from conservative clergy. Luther's old university, Wittenberg, was a bastion of opposition to pietism.

Spener pastored in Frankfort for 20 years; then Dresden for five years; and finally in Berlin, where he lived until his death. At Dresden, he grew close to August Herman Francke, a sympathetic soul and Spener's "dutiful son in the faith." In 1692, Spener helped Francke secure a place on the theology faculty of the University of Halle. It was a fateful union. Under Francke's influence, Halle became a center of pietistic influence radiating across the world.

Nicholas Zinzendorf

Pietism renewed Lutheranism in Germany and Scandinavia; and from Halle, the Rev. Henry Muhlenberg went to America to establish the Lutheran church. But pietism was not restricted by state-church boundaries. Count Nicholas Zinzendorf, a wealthy and educated nobleman who studied at Halle, founded the Moravian Church after giving sanctuary on his land to a persecuted Czech religious group called the "Moravian Brethren." This marriage of Lutheran pietism with a group that traced its theological lineage to the work of John Huss in Bohemia proved a potent mix. Moravian missionaries took their faith to the world. John Wesley encountered their powerful witness aboard his ship to Georgia in 1735 and, again, in London. Shortly after his "heart warming" experience, Wesley visited the

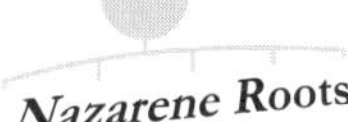


Moravian center in Herrnhut, Germany. Methodism was deeply influenced by European pietism, just as Wesleyan-Holiness churches have been.

Philip Spener, who was a sponsor at the baptism of the infant Nicholaus Zinzendorf, died in 1705. As Spener's life drew to a close, the great century of Zinzendorf and Wesley began.

## Jonathan Edwards
### *Intellect Fused with Piety*

Jonathan Edwards is often judged by one sermon, "Sinners in the Hands of an Angry God," a staple in American literature textbooks. On its basis, Edwards has been maligned as a Puritan "Elmer Gantry" who exploited the fears of credulous New Englanders desperately wanting to believe in their election to grace and heaven.

Jonathan Edwards

Historians see Edwards differently. They know him as a preacher whose dominant accent fell on God's grace reaching in love toward sinners. And they know him as America's first major theologian, an intellectual so significant that Yale University Press remains the publisher of his collected writings two centuries after his death.

Jonathan Edwards was the scion of New England Puritan preachers. His grandfather, Solomon Stoddard, was a reputable Massachusetts divine. Timothy Edwards, his father, was pastor to the Congregational church in East Windsor, Connecticut, where Jonathan was born in 1703.

> "All the graces of Christianity always go together. They so go together that where there is one, there are all, and where one is wanting, all are wanting."

In theory, New England Congregationalism was tied to the Church of England. In practice, it was an independent, self-regulated system infused with Calvinism. Its adherents regarded it as purer than the mother church in theology and government, and Edwards was steeped in this ethos.

His mind was eager. He learned Latin easily, wrote eloquent essays on nature, and entered Yale College at 13, graduating at 17. He remained two further years to study theology, then became pastor to a Presbyterian church in New York City; but the experience was unfruitful, perhaps due to his youth. In two years, he returned to Yale as senior tutor, which under the existing system, made him its chief officer and instructor.

In 1726, Edwards became the aging Stoddard's associate at Northampton, Mass. The improved salary allowed him to marry Sarah Pierrepont the next year, and he became the parish's senior pastor when Stoddard died in 1729.

The Great Awakening, rippling through America's colonies, came to New England four years later, largely through Edwards' ministry. George Whitefield, an associate of the Wesleys, was its major leader in the South, where Anglicans held sway. Theodore Frelinghuysen of the Dutch Reformed Church and Gilbert Tennant, a Presbyterian, were the key revivalists in the Middle Colonies. Edwards led the New England phase. All four were Calvinists who defended the revival against fellow church leaders, who argued that the Great Awakening's emphasis on conversion undercut Calvin's doctrine of predestination.

"Where there is love, there is also trust; and where there is a holy trust in God; there is love to God; and where there is a gracious hope, there also is a holy fear of God."

Edwards saw the revival stirrings within his parish by 1734. The tenor of Stoddard's and Edwards' preaching—focused on the "scheme of redemption"—had prepared the way. By spring 1735, over 300 had been converted in Northampton in three months. A larger church building had to be erected by 1737, the year Edwards published his *Faithful Narrative of the Surprising Work of God*. In England, the book spurred John Wesley's revivalism. In New England, Edwards' book, coupled with Whitefield's brief ministry there in 1740, spread the revival throughout the region.

The two revivalists differed. Whitefield—his voice pealing like a bell—preached extemporaneously. Edwards read his sermon manuscripts in monotone voice from the pulpit. If Whitefield could be accused justly of working up emotion, not so Edwards. The audience responded to the power of his ideas, not a quiver in his voice.

The Great Awakening's effects on New England religion were tremendous. By 1760, 150 new Congregational churches had been added and tens of thousands of new members—probably 30,000 to 40,000—were added. Baptist churches also grew rapidly.

"Grace is but glory begun, and glory is but grace perfected."

Edwards had to defend the revival from critics, particularly Boston's Charles Chauncey, who lamented the revival as Satan's wedge since new sects were generated by it and emotional excesses were many. In response, Edwards deplored emotional excesses where they had appeared, but he defended the role of emotions in conversion in his *Treatise Concerning Religious Affections* (1746), a serious spiritual and psychological study of Christian experience rooted in Lockean philosophy.

In spite of Northampton's many conversions, Edwards faced growing opposition to his continued leadership of that church, particularly when he sought to raise the standards for eligibility to receive communion. In 1850, he accepted a call to Stockbridge, a frontier community, where he ministered to Indian and white congregations alike until 1857. He penned

some of his most important writings during the Stockbridge years, among them *Freedom of the Will.*

In 1757, he succeeded his son-in-law, Aaron Burr, recently deceased, as president of Princeton in New Jersey. Burr's son, also named Aaron, joined their household. Edwards' tenure at Princeton was short-lived. He died a few months later from a failed small pox inoculation, and his wife died shortly after that.

He left a body of writings—sermons, treatises, books, and correspondence—that were unique. They reflect his enthusiasm for nature as God's handiwork and delight, his appreciation of psychology in religious understanding, and his acceptance and defense of revivalism as one of the methods through which God brings people to faith.

### George Whitefield
### ***Wayfaring Witness to England and America***

In one of history's ironies, many consider George Whitefield the 18th century's most outstanding English-language preacher. So little in his youth predicted that outcome. His parents were tavern-keepers in Gloucester, England. His father died when he was only two. And throughout childhood, Whitefield largely was unaware of Christ or creed.

George Whitefield (Age 24)

"Self- righteousness is the last idol that is rooted out of the heart."

These working-class origins, though, fitted Whitefield for the ministry he later undertook. He never forgot the social class from which he rose, nor lost his ability to appreciate the common people.

Whitefield possessed three qualities that helped him escape the poverty and complex social evils of his day: a gifted mind, an excellent voice, and a strong ambition to improve his position. He was able to enroll in school and earn scholarships. He performed menial tasks to supplement his income. His gifts for oratory and theater were recognized and encouraged by teachers. Educated people brought him into contact with the Church of England, and, at 16, he took Holy Communion for the first time.

Eventually Whitefield worked his way into Oxford University. There he met an older student from the north country named Charles Wesley. Whitefield also came under the influence of Charles' older brother, John, and joined the Holy Club—the name used by the original Oxford Methodists. Of the Holy Club's various members, only Whitefield was forced by the circumstances of his background to work his way

"It is a poor sermon that gives no offense; that neither makes the hearer displeased with himself nor with the preacher."

George Whitefield

"To preach more than half an hour, a man should be an angel himself or have angels for hearers."

through the university. The rest were supported by their families or benefactors.

Whitefield entered fully into the Holy Club's rigorous search for Christian assurance. In 1735, he became the first of the Oxford Methodists to experience the assurance of salvation. This experience galvanized him. He became an intense and effective evangelist who formed his converts into religious societies.

The Wesleys sailed for America that same year. Whitefield led the Holy Club in their absence. The Church of England ordained him a deacon in 1736, and Whitefield intended to remain at Oxford and pursue a graduate degree. His burgeoning evangelistic itinerary soon steered him down a very different path.

In a brief period of remarkable experimentation, Whitefield blazed new paths for ministry that the Wesleys would take over and adapt. It was Whitefield, for instance, who began to itinerate between London, in the east, and Bristol—a seaport on England's west coast. London and Bristol would become the two anchors of English Methodism.

Whitefield's ministry in the west extended to those in the poor mining communities around Bristol. His preaching in London and Bristol became a sensation. People crowded the churches to hear him. Printers offered to publish his sermons.

Whitefield developed a strong conviction that he should follow the Wesleys to Georgia. He was not deterred from this hope when first Charles and then John returned to England, tormented and depressed by their American adventures. He spent three months in Georgia in 1738, laying plans to establish an orphan's home. He returned to England and was ordained a priest the next year.

Whitefield first encountered open-air preaching in Wales, where he went seeking funds for his orphanage. Howell Harris, a Welsh revivalist, had begun outdoor preaching in order to attract the poor, who rarely darkened the church door. Whitefield, in turn, experimented with this method at Kingswood, a coal mining community near Bristol.

The tactic scandalized "respectable" people. In protest, parish priests began refusing Whitefield the use of their pulpits. It did not matter. Crowds flocked to hear him preach outside as readily as inside. Whitefield's following grew stronger, and a network of preaching points developed. Whitefield faced a crucial problem as he laid plans to return to Georgia and build the orphanage: What provision should he make for these people who were coming to depend on him for pastoral care?

It was only natural to invite John Wesley to visit the work in Bristol. Whitefield prevailed upon Wesley to try open-air preaching, a distasteful duty that Wesley described in his journal beginning with these words: "I submitted to be yet more vile." Nevertheless, Wesley saw, as Whitefield had, that the poor responded favorably to the preacher who would meet them on their level.

In a decision that proved fateful to all three men and to the future of Methodism, Whitefield turned over to the Wesleys the networks he had created in London and Bristol. From that point forward, the two Wesleys fused the roles of evangelist and pastor. They devoted the remainder of their lives to expanding these networks, establishing religious societies, and ministering to England's most neglected people.

> "It is an undoubted truth that every doctrine that comes from God, leads to God."

Whitefield's career moved in a different direction. He became devoted almost entirely to itinerant evangelism, moving ceaselessly between England and America, and abroad in each land. In all, he made seven trips to the American colonies, staying in the colonies for several years each time.

Whitefield emerged as the most cohesive figure in the revival known as the Great Awakening. Jonathan Edwards, the famed Congregationalist preacher, led the Awakening in New England. Gilbert Tennant, a Presbyterian, did the same in the Middle Atlantic colonies. But Whitefield traversed up and down the Atlantic coast, preaching in New England, the South, and points in between. He was the one link between the separate local phases of the Great Awakening. The orphanage in Georgia remained a principal concern throughout his itinerant ministry.

Whitefield's relationship with the Wesleys grew more complicated over time, marred by strong differences over theology. Unlike the Wesleys, Whitefield was always a Calvinist in his basic theological viewpoint.

In 1742, a conflict over predestination and the nature of Christ's atonement broke out between the Wesleyan Methodists and the smaller Calvinistic wing that looked to Whitefield, Howell Harris, and Lady Huntingdon for leadership. This argument led to a break in the friendship between Whitefield and the Wesleys. By 1750, fellowship had been restored, but the Methodist movement now existed in two parts.

The main branch was the "Wesleyan Methodist Connexion," which taught that Christ died for all and that entire sanctification was a possibility for any believer. The Calvinistic wing included the Welsh Methodists led by Harris, and, in England, a group known as "Lady Huntingdon's Connexion."

The predestination controversy flared again in the 1770s and was ongoing when Whitefield died suddenly in Massachusetts, apparently of a severe asthma attack. Memorial services were conducted for him throughout the American colonies. In England, despite the theological differences between Wesleyan and Calvinistic Methodists, John Wesley preached the funeral sermon for his old friend.

**William Wilberforce**
***Evangelical Reformer***

William Wilberforce's conversion in 1785 prefaced one of Christian history's nobler chapters. The visionary blend of piety and social reform of Wilberforce and his colleagues energized the British campaign against slavery and achieved numerous reforms.

William Willberforce

Wilberforce's colleagues were his influential neighbors whose homes ringed the city common of Clapham, outside London. They were banker Henry Thornton; lawyer James Stephen; Charles Grant and John Shore of the East India Company; rector John Venn of Clapham's Anglican church; and Zachary Macaulay, an administrator. Spiritually indebted to the Wesleys and George Whitefield, this group reshaped the evangelical wing of the Church of England. There was one other: the radical Whig politician William Smith, a Unitarian. Smith's Christology grieved the evangelicals, but they received him as a comrade in arms who shared their view that English society was suffering a moral crisis and that a revival of "true Christianity" was the antidote.

"We do not hear the Gospel much anymore in our pulpits, but we hear it in our prayers."

In Thornton's library, the group plotted strategies to make England more humane: schemes to educate the poor, reform labor laws, abolish sports that brutalized animals, open India to Christian missions, and abolish slavery. Enemies despised them as "the Saints." Later they were dubbed the "Clapham sect. "

Wilberforce was the point man. Born in 1759, he was educated at Cambridge. In 1780, he was elected to Parliament, where he was close to William Pitt, Britain's energetic young prime minister .

His conversion made Wilberforce receptive to the plea of antislavery leaders who sought a champion to bring their issue before Parliament. It would be a monumental undertaking, but Wilberforce agreed to it, earning John Wesley's unequivocal blessing, among others.

Slavery had been declared illegal in England itself, but thousands of slaves worked on the lucrative sugar plantations in the British West Indies. The industry was vital to England's economy, and slavery's supporters were entrenched. The abolitionists' strategy was first to halt the Atlantic slave trade and then kill slavery as an institution.

The campaign proceeded along two fronts: moving legislation through Parliament, and educating public opinion. Thomas Clarkson knew how to rally popular support. Stephen and Macaulay, former residents of the West Indies, marshaled key information. Macaulay had been the administrator of a Jamaican sugar plantation and had witnessed the slaves' conditions. He had a photographic memory and was an admirable researcher who was often singled out for criticism by abolition's opponents.

In Parliament, Wilberforce, Smith, and Clarkson spent months interviewing witnesses who appeared before their committee. Slave ship captains, sugar plantation owners and employees, and missionaries appeared to testify. They also received written testimony from agents in the West Indies.

> "The nature and all the circumstances of this [slave] trade are now laid open to us. We can no longer plead ignorance, we cannot evade it; . . . we may spurn it, we may kick it out of our way, but we cannot turn aside so as to avoid seeing it."

In 1789, Wilberforce introduced in the House of Commons a bill to abolish slavery. Whigs and Tories alike were split on the measure, and it was laid aside. In 1792, he introduced another bill. This one, amended to provide for gradual abolition, was passed by Commons only to fail in the House of Lords.

The French Revolution intervened. Its excesses threatened the English upper classes. Parliament grew conservative, even reactionary, and would not consider social reforms until stability returned to Europe. Further efforts seemed unfruitful until 1804 when Wilberforce and the abolitionists renewed the antislavery campaign.

The first major victory came in 1807. A new coalition controlled Parliament. A measure to end the Atlantic slave trade was introduced and passed overwhelmingly. The Clapham sect rejoiced, as did countless Quakers, Methodists, Unitarians, and others. A broad coalition of religious groups had achieved a notable success.

The struggle to free those already in slavery remained, and this victory did not come easily. The Napoleonic wars diverted public attention from the issue and hardened conservative resistance to reform. Wilberforce's round of speeches and rallies continued for years.

The time seemed right in 1821 for Wilberforce to introduce a new bill to abolish slavery. It went nowhere. Ill and losing his sight, he began grooming Thomas Buxton as his successor in the struggle. Buxton

William Willberforce

increasingly assumed Wilberforce's load. Indeed, a new generation of evangelicals assumed responsibility as the Clapham sect passed from the scene. Buxton led the united campaign when Parliament abolished slavery throughout the British empire in 1833. Wilberforce, on his deathbed, learned the news only hours before he died. Days later, a grateful nation buried him in London's Westminster Abbey.

# CHAPTER 2

# A Methodist Heritage

## Introduction

The first Nazarene missionaries sailed from America to India in 1897. Their eastward route took them to England, where they changed ships before crossing the Mediterranean. They spent one Sunday in London, attending services at the City Road Chapel, the "mother church" of all Methodism. Then they visited the nearby graves of John Wesley and his mother, Susannah. As these missionaries stood at Wesley's grave, they no doubt remembered his famous statement: "The world is my parish."

Early Nazarenes understood themselves to be part of the wider Methodist people. When evangelist C. W. Ruth wrote W. C. Wilson of Kentucky, urging him to join the Nazarenes, he emphasized that "the Nazarenes are nothing in the world but old-fashioned Methodists." Then Ruth paraphrased a sentence from the minutes of an early Methodist conference in London and reaffirmed by American Methodists in 1784: "Our business," Ruth said, "is to spread Scriptural Holiness over these lands."

Phineas Bresee reflected this viewpoint when he wrote: "We feel ourselves a part of that body of believers raised up to spread sanctified holiness over these lands, and thus that we are a part of that company who are the real successors of John Wesley and the early Methodists" (*Nazarene Messenger*, July 15, 1909: 6). J. B. Chapman also made the point in the first denominational history of the Nazarenes:

> "There was once a time when the majority of aggressive Holiness people were in the Friends or Quaker Church. At a later period, the vast majority of those who were aggressively seeking to lead men into the experience of holiness of heart as a work of grace . . . were in the Methodist Church. And while the 'Holiness Movement' has had a scope of influence which has included [non-Methodists] in various Christian lands, still Methodism in its various branches and the people who have either directly or indirectly been influenced by the Methodists, especially the early Methodists, have made by far the largest contribution to it." (J. B. Chapman, *A History of the Church of the Nazarene* [1926], pp. 13-14.)

The Nazarene Articles of Faith reflected the doctrinal and spiritual core of Wesleyan theology. For that very reason, J. B. Chapman urged all Holiness preachers to be dedicated readers and students of John Wesley's writings. But early Nazarenes also understood themselves as Methodists in structure and practice. Theologian A. M. Hills, who maintained that "the Church of the Nazarene is the fairest flower . . . in the Methodist garden," believed that the Nazarenes stood in continuity with historic Methodism in the six basic areas of superintendency, evangelism, missions, theological education, spiritual formation, and higher education.

The Wesleyan-Holiness Movement in American Methodism was the significant catalyst in the Church of the Nazarene's origins. The Holiness revival originated at the core of American Methodism's central tradition, represented by the Methodist Episcopal Church and the Methodist Episcopal Church, South—churches, once joined, that divided over the slavery issue. When the Holiness Movement arose, three other Methodist groups on American soil existed as distinct and separate from the central tradition. Two were demarked by lines of race and ethnicity: African Methodism and German Methodism. The third group can be described as democratic Methodists, represented by the Methodist Protestants, Wesleyan Methodists, and later Free Methodists.

Pastors, evangelists, and people from the three dissenting groups joined mainline Methodists as participants in the Holiness revival, which functioned as a bridge of unity between the various Methodist branches for two generations.

Then near the end of the 19th century, the Holiness Movement began to produce groups that splintered off from mainline Methodism. New denominations arose that were related to one another through common roots in the Holiness revival. In time, the Wesleyan Methodists and Free Methodists gravitated toward this camp, while the Church of the Nazarene assumed its present form as smaller Wesleyan-Holiness groups coalesced on the east coast, in the South, and then together with a group from the West.

The early Nazarenes drew members from several of the Methodist traditions. They drew their largest corps, by far, from the Methodist Episcopal churches. Phineas Bresee, Hiram F. Reynolds, W. C. Wilson, R. T. Williams, George Sharpe, Mary Lee Cagle, B. F. Haynes, C. J. Kinne, and many others were products of the central tradition. Bresee, Reynolds, and Sharpe, for instance, were ordained in the Methodist Episcopal Church and began their ministries there, while Haynes and Wilson were ministers originally in the M.E.C., South. But the Nazarenes also attracted German Methodists like C. W. Ruth, H. Orton Wiley, and the clergy couple of Theodore and Minnie Ludwig. And they attracted Methodist Protestants like evangelist Eliza Rutherford of Texas.

This chapter focuses on people in the Methodist traditions whose lives were connected to the Wesleyan-Holiness impulse. Besides the founders of Methodism, they include revivalists, sect leaders, black evangelists, and missionaries. Their witness to the religion of the warmed heart and their dedication to a gospel of Christian perfection was well-known to early Nazarene leaders.

## Charles Wesley
### *Preacher and Poet of the Evangelical Revival*

Charles Wesley

By God's grace, great things can flow from small origins. A monk in 16th-century Saxony reformed the curriculum of his university's theology department, departing radically from the typical approach of his day. In defending his new curriculum, Martin Luther launched the Protestant Reformation.

Three centuries later, a young Oxford University student wasted his first year in trivial pursuits before buckling down. The next year, in his words, "I . . . persuaded two or three young scholars to accompany me, and to observe the course of study prescribed by the Statutes of the University. This gained me the harmless nickname of 'Methodist.'"

The writer was Charles Wesley. His associates were William Morgan and Robert Kirkham. A university regulation encouraged students to form groups and mutually support one another in academic and religious pursuits. It was widely ignored, and the decision of these three to honor it led others to scorn them. But that decision resulted in the Holy Club—the first Methodist society ever—and made them the first Methodists in the world.

Charles Wesley
*(John Russell Portrait)*

Charles was the youngest son of the Anglican minister of Epworth, Samuel Wesley, and his wife, Susannah. Charles was born in 1707, one week before Christmas, and raised in a house filled with older sisters. At eight, he was sent south to London, to the Westminster School, where his oldest brother, Samuel Jr., was master. In 1727, he entered Oxford, from which another brother, John, had just taken his leave.

Preacher & Poet of the Evangelical Revival

The Holy Club became the arena for Charles Wesley's intense search for an authentic faith. Academic studies, religious devotion, and good works on behalf of the poor and imprisoned became its primary activities. It grew slowly. When John Wesley returned to Oxford later in 1729, Charles prevailed on his brother to exercise leadership of the group. Their fortunes were linked from that day forth.

Charles graduated in 1730, but stayed at Oxford to earn a master's degree and tutor younger students. Driven by a desire to find God's place for them, the Wesleys contacted James Oglethorpe, founder of the Georgia colony in British North America, about going to the frontier as missionaries to the Indians. They were accepted. Charles was appointed as Oglethorpe's personal secretary. John would serve the colony in Frederica and minister to the Indians of the area as opportunity allowed. In late 1735, a few weeks before sailing, Edmund Gibson, Bishop of London, ordained Charles as a priest in the Church of England.

The Wesleys' grand ambition to convert the Indians came to nothing. Charles, ill-suited to secretarial tasks, grew ill and depressed. He was back in England before the end of 1736. John's complicated relationship with a young woman and general opposition to his religious rigor ended his ministry in Georgia as well.

Still, an important contact had been made. On the voyage to America, the Wesleys first met the Moravians, a German Pietist sect, who spoke in personal terms of being "justified by faith" and of the assurance of salvation. Their strong and vibrant faith seemed to mock

the Puritanical and legalistic approach that John and Charles took to religion.

In London, Charles and John pursued contacts with Moravians there. One, Peter Böhler, exercised a strong influence on them. And so through Moravian influence, the Wesley brothers both experienced evangelical grace in May 1738—Charles on the 21st while praying in the home of Thomas Bray, and John on the 24th at a religious meeting on Aldersgate Street.

Charles Wesley
*(William Gush Portrait)*

The remainder of Charles Wesley's life fell into three stages. He itinerated throughout the British Isles on behalf of the Methodist cause until his marriage to Sarah Gwynne in 1749. After their marriage, the couple settled in Bristol, an Atlantic seaport, and a primary stronghold of Methodism. Charles gave oversight to the Methodist societies in the Bristol area for the next 22 years.

In 1771, Charles moved his family to London in order to improve his sons' prospects. There, he exercised oversight of the Methodist societies in greater London, playing the same role he had in Bristol. After the New Chapel was built on City Road in 1778, Charles gave it his special attention until his death 10 years later.

Charles was a compulsive writer of verse throughout his life. This talent was shared with John, their father Samuel, and with Charles' own sons. After his conversion, most of Charles Wesley's verse was religious in nature. Great themes of grace, faith, and sanctification run through many of them, but he also delighted in writing Eucharistic poetry that celebrated the sacrament of the Lord's Supper. As Maldwyn Edwards has written, it was in these poems and hymns that Charles Wesley made his "greatest contribution to the universal Church."

The publication of hymnbooks was one of the great joint collaborations of the Wesley brothers. *Hymns and Sacred Poems* (1739) gained wide circulation, and an American edition even appeared the next year. Others followed over the years, but their greatest effort was their 1780 hymnal, *A Collection of Hymns for the Use of the People Called Methodists.* Over half of its 525 hymns were written by Charles. Many regard it as the greatest hymnal ever published. Indeed, some rank it with the *Book of Common Prayer* as the two most important books of religious devotion ever published in England.

Charles Wesley—this poet and preacher of the Evangelical Revival—died in London on March 29, 1788. An earnest Christian, his life still inspires all who aspire to holy living.

**John Wesley**
***Founder of Methodism***

John Wesley
*(Hunter Portrait)*

"By holiness I mean, not fasting, or bodily austerity, or any other external means of improvement, but that inward temper to which all these are subservient, a renewal of soul in the image of God."

Young John nearly died as fire consumed Epworth's parsonage, but stout men formed a human ladder reaching to the second floor, where the boy stood solemnly at the window. Strong hands snatched him before the fire could, leading Susannah Wesley to remark that her middle son was "a brand plucked from the burning." Thereafter, nothing shook her faith that God had a distinct purpose for his life.

John Wesley was born in Epworth, England, in 1703. He was the 15th child of Samuel Wesley, the rector (local priest), and Susannah. An argument drove husband and wife apart for a few months. John, it is often remarked, was the fruit of their reconciliation. In all, Susannah gave birth to 19 children; only 9 survived infancy. At his birth, several sisters separated John from his older brother, Samuel, Jr. Charles, born 1707, came last.

John's youth in Epworth was happy and filled with the constant presence of five sisters, but the household was also regimented, for Susannah Wesley believed in discipline. How else could she manage such a large family? She taught her children to read and every week spent an hour of personal time with each.

In 1714, John was sent to London to attend Charterhouse, a private school for children of people like his father: educated, dignified, but poor. In 1720, he entered Christ Church College at Oxford, graduating with his bachelor's degree in 1724. At first, he spent many frivolous hours at Oxford, but finally he buckled down.

The year 1725 was pivotal. Wesley became serious about his inner religious life. He read Jeremy Taylor's *Holy Living and Dying*, Thomas à Kempis' *The Imitation of Christ*, and William Law's *A Serious Call to a Devout and Holy Life.* Each book made an imprint on his thinking and shaped his theology of sanctification. He determined to follow his father and older brother into the Anglican ministry, preached his first sermon, and was ordained a deacon late in the year.

He was elected a fellow of Lincoln College the next year. This was a university post. It required him to teach logic and classics to undergraduates for part of the year, but freed him for study or parish ministry for many other months. Bishop Potter ordained him a priest in the Church of England in 1728.

For several months, he worked as his father's assistant at Wroote, a hamlet near Epworth. He returned to Oxford in 1729 to discover the Holy Club, formed by his brother Charles.

John quickly became its natural leader, leading it for nearly six years. Others derided them as "Bible moths" and "Methodists." They accepted the last name as a testament to their methodical and disciplined approach to education and faith. Through a mutual process, but under John's guidance, Methodism's basic unit and character was formed at Oxford. To be a Methodist was to belong to a religious society that promoted a right relationship with God through common prayer, Bible readings, mutual exhortation, and discipline. The study of Scripture led Wesley and the other Oxford Methodists to believe that "faith without works is dead," so they reached out to the poor, the destitute, and the prisoners, ministering to body and spirit alike as there was need. Though Methodism's character was shaped at Oxford, it did not spread as a movement until 1739.

John Wesley
*(Salisbury Portrait)*

In the intervening years, John remained at Oxford until 1735, when he and Charles went to Georgia as missionaries. They discovered that they did not fit into frontier society and returned to England greatly frustrated. The brothers were also troubled and sought a deep evangelical faith that each could call his own.

John found this faith while attending a meeting of the Aldersgate Society, one of several dozen religious societies in London. While someone read aloud from Martin Luther's *Preface to the Book of Romans,* Wesley found his heart "strangely warmed" and received a deep assurance of faith. He later described this change: his faith before Aldersgate was that of a servant; his faith afterwards was that of a son.

In many ways, everything that Wesley experienced to this point—education, the Holy Club, the Georgia sojourn, and evangelical conversion—was preparation for the next stage of life. At age 36, he took over George Whitefield's preaching points and religious societies in the vicinity of Bristol. At first, John simply imitated Whitefield by pastoring the societies and preaching outdoors to the throngs of workers going to and from their labors. However in time, John and Charles began planting new societies around Bristol and then in other places. Within a few months, London, Bristol, and Newcastle became three points on a triangular circuit that Wesley traveled regularly, organizing new Methodist societies along the circuit. Then the societies spread into other parts of the United Kingdom. The Methodist movement became Wesley's parish, and he a spiritual shepherd to those who joined the societies.

John Wesley
*(painted by John Michael Williams in 1742)*

John Wesley
*(Russel Portrait)*

Why did Methodism grow into a mass movement when similar English religious societies did not? There are many reasons: Charles Wesley's hymns, John Wesley's preaching, his knack for organization, his total dedication to the pastoral care of his growing flock, his attention to spiritual formation, the breadth of their theology, and the conscientious decision to take the gospel to the poor.

The decision to take the gospel to the poor was an idea developed at Oxford. Applied on a large scale, it became the dynamic behind Methodism's phenomenal growth. This set the Methodist societies apart from the other religious societies of the day, which were earnest but not so self-replicating. John Wesley understood the great religious challenge of his time. People had migrated from the English farms. Some had crossed the Atlantic to the American colonies. Others congregated in England's burgeoning cities. Parish boundaries were obsolete, but Anglican bishops sensed no need for building new churches or creating new parishes where people now congregated. Wesley did not understand this neglect, and he was deeply moved by the plight of those who were like sheep without a shepherd. He decided that Methodist societies would form a network beneath formal church structures, bringing people to faith, making them accountable to one another for their conduct and discipleship, and pressing upon them the biblical call to holiness.

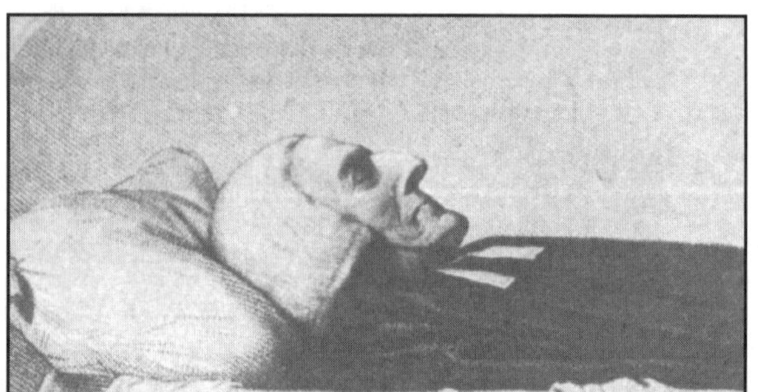
John Wesley
*(Ridley's Sketch of Wesley as he lay in state)*

John Wesley's reading in 1725 had born remarkable fruit. The theme of holiness that ran through the writings of Kempis, Law, and Taylor was a theme upon which he meditated all those years. Several sources document how he developed his hermeneutic of Christian holiness. *A Plain Account of Christian Perfection* is one of these. In it, he defended his theology of holiness by showing how it was grounded on Scripture, experience, and Christian tradition. He further described the various stages of his life that led to this understanding. For many years, Nazarene candidates for ordination were required to read the *Plain Account* and enter into Wesley's thinking. The minutes of the annual meetings that John Wesley convened beginning in the mid-1740s also show how Wesley's theological commitments were developed.

John Wesley
*(Jackson Portrait)*

Wesley's mature thought on holiness positioned him in the Protestant tradition of justification by grace through faith. Further, he affirmed that

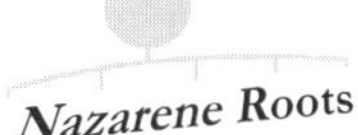


sanctification is likewise by grace through faith, that entire sanctification is instantaneous, and that the instant of entire sanctification is both preceded and followed by a progressive sanctification. The progressive work *before* entire sanctification is a process of divine love "excluding sin." Once sin is excluded wholly, the progressive work is the growth of the thoroughly sanctified Christian's ever enlarging capacity to love. Wesley held that love of God and neighbor is the ultimate sign of holy love reigning in a believer's heart.

John Wesley
*(Romney Portrait)*

In much the same way that Paul the apostle or the writer of John's Gospel could claim to be "the theologian of love," so John Wesley could make that claim. He believed that God's essential character is love. Since the erasure of sin in human lives means "the renewal of soul in the image of God," it also means that the sanctified believer develops the capacity to love as God loves. For Wesley, "evangelical faith" and "evangelical love" are linked so tightly together that one is not present in human life without the other. The faith that burns in a Christian's heart purifies it and fills it with love. Thus, the evangelistic love of God and neighbor unites heart and hand in service to God and to our fellows.

"As our bodies are strengthened by bread and wine, so are our souls by these tokens of the body and blood of Christ. This is the food of our souls. This gives strength to perform our duty, and leads us on to perfection."

Much more could be said: how Wesley utilized lay preachers to do the work that Anglican clergy would not do; how Methodism became a missionary movement; how the Methodists used Sunday schools to provide basic education and religious instruction to the poor; how *The Christian Library* was formed to put basic religious literature in the hands of the thousands whom they taught to read; how Wesley founded *The Arminian Magazine* to provide theological guidance and to publish the testimonies to the work of God within the united societies; how his collected writings fill dozens of volumes; and how, on his deathbed, he wrote his very last letter to William Wilberforce, urging the latter to devote his life to ending slavery in the British Empire.

Until the end of his life, John Wesley traveled constantly throughout the United Kingdom, preaching the gospel of grace and holiness and shepherding the Methodist societies. Unlike Charles, who married, quit traveling, and settled into a life of domestic comfort, John remained the circuit-riding pastor, an inspiration and example to all the other Methodist preachers. Every romantic attachment that Wesley formed was ultimately undermined by the sense that the Methodist people had the first right to his loyalty, and when he married late in life, it proved a mistake, resulting in an unhappy marriage for both partners.

In truth, the Methodist movement was his bride and the societies were his children. He filled the roles of pastor, evangelist, theologian, and social reformer, and he filled each role well. He died in 1791 and is buried in London behind the City Road Chapel.

### The Wesleyan Theological Tradition
#### *John Wesley's Extended Influence on the Nazarenes*

"Every preacher of full salvation should make John Wesley and his works a fundamental study," advised J. B. Chapman the year before he died. This mature judgment was based on the practice of a lifetime and wide experience as a pastor, editor, and general superintendent.

It resonated with Phineas Bresee's heart-felt conviction, expressed many years earlier, that Nazarenes "feel ourselves a part of that body of believers raised up to spread sanctified holiness over these lands, and thus that we are a part of that company who are the real successors of John Wesley and the early Methodists."

James Arminius

The spread of scriptural holiness was, indeed, Methodism's avowed aim. The minutes of an early Methodist conference convened by John Wesley record the following question and answer: "Q. What may we reasonably believe to be God's design in raising up the Preachers called Methodists? A. Not to form any new sect; but to reform the nation, particularly the Church; and to spread scriptural holiness over the land." Forty years later, American Methodists organized their own denomination in Baltimore, Maryland. The same question elicited this response: "A. To reform the Continent; and to spread scriptural Holiness over these Lands."

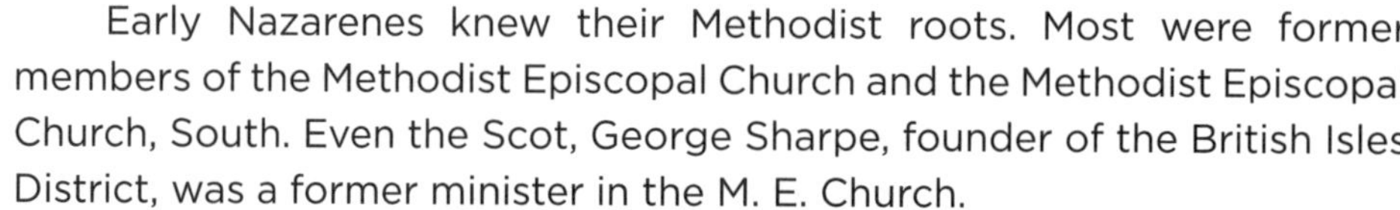

Early Nazarenes knew their Methodist roots. Most were former members of the Methodist Episcopal Church and the Methodist Episcopal Church, South. Even the Scot, George Sharpe, founder of the British Isles District, was a former minister in the M. E. Church.

Those who entered Nazarene ranks from non-Methodist backgrounds acknowledged the type of church they were joining. "Scratch a real Nazarene, and you will touch an original Methodist; skin a genuine Methodist, and behold a Nazarene!" wrote E. F. Walker, a former Presbyterian. Theologian A. M. Hills, who came to the Nazarenes from the Congregational Church, extolled the Methodist inheritance, claiming that the Nazarenes constituted "the fairest flower . . . in the Methodist garden, the most promising ecclesiastical daughter the prolific Mother Methodism has ever given to the world."

Wesleyan identity was nurtured deliberately in the early years through the Course of Study, a list of books over which ministers were examined before ordination. Until 1944, ordinands were required to read one of the major biographies of Wesley. Until 1932, they also read a selection of his sermons and J. A. Wood's *Christian Perfection, As Taught by John Wesley*, a 400-page compilation of Wesley's writings on holiness drawn from his different works.

Books by other Methodist authors filled the early Course of Study. One vital area was systematic theology, a study in the structure of Christian thought. Methodist theologians John Miley and Thomas Ralston dominated the reading requirement in systematic theology until 1940, providing the vast majority of Nazarene ministers a basic orientation to Christian theology in this period.

The requirements were designed to nurture a Wesleyan identity among Nazarene ministers and keep the church on a path of continuity with its spiritual and theological inheritance.

> "I am appalled to discover how far from Wesley we are; and I, for one, am praying that God will help us to find the way back."
> J. Glenn Gould

### A Wesleyan-Arminian Tradition

It was a rich inheritance, indeed.

During the Protestant Reformation, the Church of England's reformers tilted strongly toward Calvinism. In its rigid forms, Calvinism insists that God preordains some people to salvation and others to damnation; argues that Christ's atonement for sin is restricted to those whom God pre-elected to salvation; and declares that the recipient of justifying grace can never lose his or her salvation.

James Arminius took a different view in his protest against the hard-line Calvinism of the Dutch Reformed Church, in which he was a minister. He broke through Calvinist rigidity and appropriated a fresh understanding of the gospel. He understood Scripture to teach that Christ's atonement is an available remedy for the sins of all people, and that any person can trust in Christ for salvation and be saved. Further, he held that the precious gift of saving grace can be lost by severe or persistent sin and must be nurtured by daily living through Christ.

Anglican bishops and scholars like William Laud and Lancelot Andrewes took a similar position within the Church of England. By 1661, Calvinists were leaving the Church of England for the Presbyterian and Congregational churches. Though Calvinism had declined, it retained influence in parts of the Church of England in John Wesley's day. And this became a point of contention in early Methodism. John and Charles

Wesley embraced the Arminian perspective; their co-worker, George Whitefield, embraced Calvinism. As a result, Wesley and Whitefield engaged in several controversies over doctrine that split early Methodism into two camps.

Wesley's periodical, founded in 1778, was *The Arminian Magazine*. Its title signified his basic theological framework. His doctrine of Christian perfection, which the Calvinistic Methodists did not share at all, was set within the Arminian framework.

Thus, the Wesleyan revival was also a revival of Arminianism, especially in America, where Calvinism dominated when the Methodists arrived on the scene. Undaunted by their minority status, the Methodists set about evangelizing the American people, and by 1850 they constituted America's largest denomination.

The Wesleyan theological tradition was shaped by a number of Methodist writers in 19th-century England and America. These included theologians Richard Watson, Thomas Burt Pope, Ralston, and Miley. Nazarene theologian H. Orton Wiley picked up this theological agenda in his three-volume *Christian Theology,* which first appeared in 1940. By 1960, Wiley was considered by many to be the foremost exponent of Arminian theology in America.

**A Wesleyan-Holiness Church**

Chapman recommended the careful study of Wesley's works because they contained solid holiness theology. He knew, too, that theological roots were indispensable.

The 19th- and 20th-century Holiness Movement was hardly monolithic. The Holiness revival readily crossed denominational lines and brought Christians of differing beliefs together in mass revival meetings, where the experience of a second work of divine grace was earnestly sought. And it was here, in the realm of Christian experience, that the Holiness revival found its true unity. But the modern Holiness Movement carved four distinct channels. The Nazarenes fit naturally in only one of these.

*The Wesleyan-Holiness stream* developed from the Holiness revival within mainline Methodism. Two sources originally sparked it in the 1830s. The first was Rev. Timothy Merritt's advocacy through his periodical, *The Guide to Christian Perfection*, published in Boston.

The other was Methodist layperson Phoebe Palmer's steady hand as leader of the Tuesday Meeting for the Promotion of Holiness in New York City. Palmer generated widespread interest through her remarkable

career as a Methodist class leader, author, editor, lay preacher, and humanitarian. Merritt and Palmer were life-long students of Wesley's writings, but Palmer's affinity with Wesley was also personal: his preaching had persuaded her father, Henry Worrall, to join the Methodist cause in England. Years later in America, Palmer's sense of personal connection to Methodism's founder was strong.

A third step further spurred the Holiness revival in Methodism. In 1867, Methodist clergy organized the National Camp Meeting Association for the Promotion of Holiness at Vineland, New Jersey. Better known as the National Holiness Association, the organization remained closely tied to the Methodist Episcopal Church. Phineas Bresee served as one of its officers in the 1890s, and Hiram Reynolds was an officer in one of its affiliates, the Vermont Holiness Association.

Along America's eastern seaboard, then, a strong movement developed to lift Wesley's doctrine of Christian perfection to the same place of centrality in American Methodism that it had long held among British Methodists.

*The Oberlin Holiness Movement* also took shape in the 1830s, promoted by the religion faculty of Oberlin College in Ohio. Theology teacher Charles G. Finney, the most noted 19th-century revivalist before the Civil War, was at the core of this movement. But Finney minimized original sin, regarded free will as a human capacity rather than a divinely bestowed gift, and emphasized entire sanctification as a consecration of the self rather than as God's gracious act of cleansing from sin. His theology reflected popular American notions of self-reliance far more readily than Wesleyans could ever accept.

The *Keswick Holiness Movement* opened the third channel of Holiness influence. It originated in England through the annual Keswick Convention, first held in 1875. Its theology was diffused across America in the 1880s by D. L. Moody's associates, who went to England to convert Englishmen, and were, ironically, converted by Englishmen into proponents of a "higher Christian life." Keswick Holiness theology was fitted for moderate Calvinists. Its advocates viewed the "second work of grace" as "victory over sin" and spiritual power, but shunned the idea of purity or cleansing from sin.

The fourth stream, *Pentecostal Holiness*, originated in the early 20th century. Its proponents broke off from the Holiness Movement's Wesleyan wing and taught three distinct and successive works of divine grace: justification, entire sanctification, and baptism of the Holy Spirit. Further, they regarded speaking in tongues as "the initial evidence" of Holy Spirit baptism and tied this to the third work of grace.

Collectively the four streams constituted the modern "holiness movement." Each stream taught a "second work of divine grace" in the Christian's life subsequent to regeneration, but each stream placed its doctrine of "a second blessing" in a different and unique theological package.

The American Holiness Movement was a hodgepodge, then, of theological ideas. Nazarene theology, on the other hand, could hardly afford to be that.

To come more clearly to the point, Article X (Entire Sanctification) in the Church of the Nazarene's Articles of Faith is not an isolated doctrine. It is part of the *ordo salutis* ("order of salvation"). It forms one part of a web of related doctrines—Articles V through X—whose structures inform and support one another. In these six articles of faith, an occasional word represents the specific vocabulary of the 19th-century Holiness Movement. Yet, each of Articles V through X is distinctly Wesleyan-Arminian in its language and meaning. It was John Wesley who worked out the basic thrust of each article, while the 19th-century Holiness Movement relied on his theological direction. Each of these Articles reflects his distinctive imprint. As a package, they comprise the doctrinal core of his preaching.

The 300th anniversary of John Wesley's birth occurred in 2003. Since then, it has been appropriate for Nazarenes to reflect on the life of one whose ministry is foundational for our life together. Perhaps it is also time to take Chapman's advice to heart and "make John Wesley and his works a fundamental study."

## Francis Asbury
### *Founder of American Methodism*

Francis Asbury was one of eight missionaries that John Wesley, sent to the British colonies in North America. Wesley sent them in pairs. Asbury, in the second pair, was sent to be a circuit preacher. He is revered two centuries later as the founder of American Methodism.

Asbury was born near Birmingham, England, in 1745. His only sibling died as a baby. He was reading the Scriptures by 10, though he lacked formal education. He became a blacksmith's apprentice, but experienced

an evangelical conversion soon afterward. The man to whom he was bound, a Methodist, recognized that Asbury was gifted for ministry and allowed him to break their contract. Asbury became a young lay preacher, gaining experience and a far different kind of apprenticeship under John Wesley's watchful eye.

Francis Asbury
*(A. H. Ritchie Portrait)*

Asbury was 26 and had served five circuits before the fateful 1771 Methodist conference in Bristol. Wesley appealed for preachers to go to America and serve the religious societies that immigrant Methodists from England and Ireland had organized. These societies had local leaders, but no full-time workers to build them up and expand Methodism's work. Asbury answered this appeal. He soon was aboard ship, never to see his native land again.

He reached Philadelphia in October. He discovered that the preachers sent earlier tended to stay in one location, like parish priests. Asbury rejected this strategy. Wesley's strategy for the British Isles was for the preachers to itinerate, or move about, preaching in different locations and exchanging assignments frequently. Asbury was determined to follow his mentor's model, though others might not.

His first year was spent preaching and nurturing societies on Staten Island and northern New Jersey. He spent the next in Maryland. Through the combined efforts of Asbury and others, the societies multiplied, their members increased, and several Americans joined the ranks of the lay preachers.

Francis Asbury

Thomas Rankin arrived in 1773, appointed by Wesley to lead the Methodists in America. He remained for five years, and Rankin and Asbury came to represent contrasting styles in leadership. Rankin reflected Wesley's own style—leadership from the top down. In politics, he was strongly loyal to the British crown.

Nevertheless, Asbury was being changed by the American environment and the spirit of the colonists he shepherded. He came to understand the democratic aspirations propelling the colonies to confrontation with the English monarchy.

Asbury and the American-born preachers gave Rankin their respect, but the American Revolution proved a watershed between American and British Methodism. Once the war was underway, Rankin and Wesley's other appointees returned to England—except Asbury, who alone cast his lot with the colonists.

All of America's churches lost members during the American Revolution, except the Methodists. Under Asbury's guidance, the membership

Francis Asbury
*(Frank Salisbury Portrait)*

of the Methodist societies increased from under 5,000 at the war's beginning to nearly 14,000 by 1783. The number of preachers tripled to over 80.

Asbury faced a serious crisis as the war ground to a conclusion. Lay preachers were not authorized to administer the sacraments. The Methodist movement was still technically a part of the Church of England, but the Anglican priests who could administer the sacraments had fled to England.

The Methodist preachers in the South met in Fluvanna County, Virginia, in 1780. They decided to ordain one another to the ministry and offer the sacraments to the Methodist members at large. Asbury, unable to attend, was dismayed. The preachers in the North had resisted this step. Would the Methodist movement in America split? Asbury attended the Southern conference the next year and persuaded its preachers to stop administering the sacraments until the entire company of preachers could decide the issue as one body.

Francis Asbury's ordination

Back in England, Wesley also was concerned about the Methodists in America. Even after the war ended, the Church of England was slow to send priests to the newly independent states. Wesley felt that emergency ministers were needed. In 1784, he authorized Thomas Coke—a fellow priest in the Church of England—to ordain Asbury to the ministry. On his own authority, Wesley also ordained several lay preachers to the ministry and sent them to America with Coke. He instructed Coke and Asbury to be "general superintendents" of American Methodists.

Coke's party arrived in America and a conference was scheduled for late December. Wesley had intended that the American Methodists have their own organization. He had not envisioned that it would be a separate church. Yet, in the spirit of America's new-found independence, the "Christmas Conference" founded the first Methodist denomination in the world.

Asbury refused to accept Wesley's appointment as general superintendent unless the whole conference of preachers approved it. They did, and only then did Asbury consent to it. He was ordained deacon, elder, and general superintendent on three successive days. The Christmas Conference authorized a book of order—*The Discipline*—and an order of worship.

Francis Asbury

The Americans also approved Coke as a general superintendent, but he was "too English," never completely accepted, and visited America sporadically until his death. It was Asbury who exercised the reins of leadership in the new church.

Bishop Asbury's life was driven (in Albert Outler's words) by "a monomania for mission." He expected the Methodist preachers to itinerate and set an example as an itinerant bishop, traveling constantly, preaching daily, encouraging the work, and presiding at conferences. He became a well-known visitor to the camp meetings along Maryland's shore, the mountains of North Carolina, and New England's cities. He crossed the Appalachian mountains repeatedly and was probably the most widely traveled American of his day.

To sinners, he preached a simple message of repentance and trust in Christ. To the Methodists, he preached the necessity of a life of holiness before God and one another. Asbury was convinced of the accountability of Christians to one another. Thus, he insisted that the Methodists in America plant religious societies modeled after Wesley's societies in England, where lay class leaders helped the members in their spiritual development.

Asbury died in 1816 and was buried in Baltimore. At the time of his death, there were nearly a quarter million Methodists in America, served by some 2,000 ministers.

### Jarena Lee and Julia Foote
### *Sisters of the Cross*

Histories of the Holiness Movement generally suffer by ignoring the role of African-Americans in proclaiming Christian holiness. Sources on black participation in the 19th-century Holiness Movement, though rare, do exist. The stories of Jarena Lee and Julia Foote—reclaimed by specialists in African-American studies—should also be reclaimed by the Holiness churches.

Jarena Lee

Richard Allen

**Jarena Lee**

Jarena Lee was born in Cape May, New Jersey, in 1783. At seven, she was sent 60 miles from home to work for a rich family. After reaching adulthood, she made her way to Philadelphia, where Richard Allen, founder of the African Methodist Episcopal Church, was a strong influence upon her conversion.

Several months later, a man visited Lee and inquired about her spiritual welfare. She later wrote: "He inquired if the Lord had justified my soul. I answered yes. He then asked if he had sanctified me. I answered no; that I did not know what that was. He then undertook to instruct me further in the knowledge of the Lord respecting this blessing." She sought and experienced the grace of entire sanctification.

Several years passed until Lee sensed a new leading of the Spirit—a call to preach. She shared this with Richard Allen, who told her that she might be useful in exhorting sinners to repentance or conducting women's prayer meetings. The Methodist *Discipline* did not permit women to preach, and Allen hesitated to break new ground. Lee was relieved by this news; but after returning home, she was again burdened by the call to preach.

In 1811, she married Joseph Lee, pastor of a Methodist society in Snow Hill, outside Philadelphia. Joseph died six years later, leaving Jarena to raise two infant children.

Eight years after approaching Allen, Lee restated her case to him. This time, Allen authorized her to conduct a prayer meeting in her house. Within weeks, the flock that gathered for prayer was large enough to fill her small house.

A few weeks later, she attended Bethel A.M.E. Church in Philadelphia. The preacher read from the book of Jonah. On impulse, Lee leapt to her feet and cried out that she felt like Jonah, that God had called her years earlier, and she still had not carried out her commission. The audience was shocked at her outburst, but Bishop Allen stood and told the congregation that Lee's testimony was true. Lee later wrote that Allen's "remarks greatly strengthened me."

The following Sunday, in the house of a friend, and to a congregation of only five, Lee preached her first sermon. A few days later, she began a revival meeting in another friend's home that lasted for several months.

Lee's ministry began in earnest after this. At first, she preached only in homes throughout the Philadelphia area. Eventually, she conducted services in court houses and churches. She never became a pastor, nor

was she ever ordained to the ministry, but for the remainder of her life—some 30 more years—she performed the work of an evangelist.

Her preaching took her back to her birthplace in Cape May, where her elderly mother still lived, and to Long Island, where she preached in a barn to a racially integrated congregation that included physicians and lawyers. She preached occasionally in Bethel A.M.E. Church in Philadelphia—"mother church" of the A.M.E. denomination—and in many other places. She was active in the crusade against slavery and in the movement to give women rights within the Christian church.

Christian holiness was a frequent theme of her preaching. She wrote about an incident that occurred in the early 1820s: "I now traveled to Cecil County, Md., and the first evening spoke to a large congregation. The pastor afterwards baptized some adult persons—and we all experienced the cleansing and purifying power. We had a baptism within and without."

Near the end of her life, Lee recorded these and other incidents in her autobiography, *Religious Experience and Journal of Mrs. Jarena Lee* (1849). She died a year or so later.

### Julia Foote

Lee's ministry was in full bloom when Julia Foote was born in 1823 in Schenectady, New York. Her parents, freed slaves, had earlier made their way North. Foote was converted at 15 and united with the A.M.E. Church. Soon afterwards, she sought and found the grace of entire sanctification.

After marriage, she and her husband moved to Boston. She united with a congregation of the A.M.E. Zion Church, a denomination similar to but separate from the A.M.E. Church. She became involved in visiting "the poor and forsaken ones" in homes and hospitals.

She opposed the idea of women preaching, and so it was with surprise when—in the late 1840s—she began sensing a divine call to just this work. She struggled with the call, but eventually accepted it, though her own pastor discouraged her and the congregation expelled her for doing so.

In the spring of 1849, Foote lost both her husband and her father to death. This harsh blow affected her ministry. Childless and single again, her ministry (like Jarena Lee's) developed an ever-widening circle that carried her from eastern Canada to California, though New York, Ohio, and Michigan were the center of her activities. In spite of prejudice against her ministry, she found open doors nonetheless from both A.M.E. and A.M.E. Zion congregations.

Christian holiness was an indispensable theme in Foote's sermons. Her autobiography is laced with the theme, and its last chapter is "How to Obtain Sanctification." At least one edition of the biography was published by a Holiness press. Her sermon on "Christian Perfection" has recently been republished in a new significant study of black women preachers.

The A.M.E. Zion eventually affirmed her call to ministry. From 1884 until her death in 1901, Foote lived with the family of one of her bishops. In 1894, she became the first woman ordained a deacon in her denomination, and in 1900, she was the second A.M.E. Zion woman to be ordained an elder.

## Orange Scott
### *The Abolitionist Temperament*

The Wesleyan Methodist Church was founded in 1843 by a circle of men who emerged as political activists in the Methodist Episcopal Church. Orange Scott was the central figure of this circle. Their goal: to unite "the religion of the heart" with the cause of an oppressed race.

Orange Scott

Orange Scott was born in Vermont in 1800 into a family of migrant farm workers. Poorly clothed, he rarely saw the inside of a church, but he became serious about religion in early adulthood.

He was self-taught, like many who lacked formal education, and began diligently to study the Bible. He was converted in a Methodist camp meeting, joined a Methodist church, and soon was appointed leader of a class meeting. In time, he was called to the ministry. The New England Conference ordained Scott and made him a circuit-riding preacher.

Scott soon demonstrated that he had overcome the handicap of his rude beginnings. Bishops appointed him repeatedly to serve as presiding elder (district superintendent) in Massachusetts and Rhode Island. Colleagues elected him three times as their delegate to the General Conference of the M. E. Church.

Scott was drawn into the crusade to abolish slavery in the early 1830s. A growing determination to advocate the slaves' cause soon resulted in direct conflict with his bishops and the majority sentiment within his denomination.

Scott began preaching anti-slavery sermons, writing anti-slavery articles, and giving anti-slavery speeches. He purchased nearly 100 subscriptions to William Lloyd Garrison's radical abolitionist magazine, *The Liberator,* so that each Methodist minister in New England would

receive it. Between 1834 and 1836, Scott and another minister, La Roy Sunderland, organized anti-slavery societies in the church's New England, New York, and New Hampshire Conferences.

Scott, Sunderland, and other abolitionists were inspired by the fact that John Wesley had written his final letter in opposition to slavery within the British Empire. However, the attitude of the M.E. Church's establishment was not so favorable. American Methodists had been divided on the issue from the beginning. The "Christmas Conference" establishing the M.E. Church in 1784 had taken a stand against slavery, but the following year, Methodists in Southern states had rejected the first General Conference's position and threatened the church with schism. An uneasy truce had remained in place ever since.

Successive bishops were committed to a policy of "don't rock the boat." Many black Methodists finally had forsaken the M.E. Church in the 1810s and 1820s, setting up the African Methodist Episcopal Church and the African Methodist Episcopal Zion Church. Then Scott and his associates came along in the 1830s to once again disturb the church's uneasy peace.

The M.E. Church's official press reflected establishment thinking, so the abolitionists needed their own papers. Sunderland edited *Zion's Watchman* in New York. Luther Lee, another associate, edited and published the *New England Christian Advocate* in Massachusetts.

Scott took the cause to the floor of the 1836 General Conference as a public spokesman for two ministers accused of slandering fellow clergy in the course of their abolitionists activities.

Moreover, in the ensuing debate a fraternal delegate representing British Methodism urged the General Conference to maintain the principle of opposing slavery, even if they were not going to enforce it. British Methodists had consistently worked to end slavery in the British Empire from Wesley's death until their objective was attained in 1833. But Southern delegates were offended by the Englishman's heart-felt remarks, and the General Conference voted not to include them in the official minutes. Scott spoke out heatedly in favor of retaining the remarks in the record.

Bishops became more active thereafter in disciplining anti-slavery activism among Methodist clergy. Some abolitionist clergy, including Orange Scott, were appointed to less desirable churches than their experience and years of service to their conferences warranted. At least one annual conference terminated all candidates for ministry who harbored abolitionist sympathies.

Scott and other abolitionists began to view their bishops as enforcers of a corrupt ecclesiasticism and eventually viewed the very office of bishop as undesirable and oppressive. They increasingly advocated the reform of church government as well.

The General Conference of 1840 proved to be a brick wall for the abolitionist cause. Scott withdrew from active ministry soon afterward and began publishing *The True Wesleyan* in 1842. It called for a new brand of Methodism unswervingly aligned on the side of the slaves, and for a church without bishops.

In 1843, sympathetic ministers and laymen met to plot the lines for a new body, the Wesleyan Methodist Connection of America. The word "connection" was important; it implied that they were a religious body but not "an ecclesiasticism." By 1844, there were 15,000 members.

The new church was committed to an egalitarian agenda across the board. It opposed slavery. It required equal lay and clergy representation at each annual and general conference. Each General Conference elected its own president, but no single official or body of officials exercised authority between General Conferences. Each of six annual conferences would appoint ministers to churches through a democratic method—a special appointing committee composed equally of laity and clergy. Each annual conference would elect its own presiding elder for a term of one year.

The denomination's egalitarianism was eventually reflected in still other ways. Luther Lee emerged as a staunch advocate of ordaining women and preached the ordination sermon when Antoinette Brown, a Congregationalist, became the first woman of record ordained in America. A Wesleyan Methodist church in Seneca Falls, New York, became the setting where the first women's rights convention in America was held. Wesleyan Methodists also sent bold abolitionist preachers into areas of the slave-holding South, especially North Carolina, to organize societies there.

Scott worked diligently to build the Wesleyan Methodist Connection by traveling among the six annual conferences and lifting up the religious and social work of his church. *The True Wesleyan* was purchased from him in 1844 to become the denominational paper. This action lifted some of his burden, but tuberculosis took Scott's life in 1847.

Lee and a majority of Wesleyan Methodists returned to the Methodist Episcopal Church after the Civil War. The slavery issue was now resolved. Some Wesleyan Methodists opposed this reunion, however, and in the 1870s Adam Crooks led the remaining Wesleyan Methodists to a new

sense of purpose through commitment to the Wesleyan-Holiness revival. In the 1920s, Herald of Holiness editor J. B. Chapman called repeatedly for a merger of Nazarene, Free Methodist, Wesleyan Methodist, and Pilgrim Holiness denominations. It was not to be. But in 1968 Wesleyan Methodists merged with the Pilgrim Holiness people to create the present-day Wesleyan Church.

### Phoebe Palmer
***Mother of the Wesleyan-Holiness Revival***

On the day of Phoebe Palmer's funeral, thousands took to the New York City streets to memorialize the life of one of the most unique women in American mainline religion. She had championed the right of women to preach. She had helped organize social work in the New York City slums. She had written several books and edited a periodical with one of the largest distributions of her day. And she had given birth to six children and, to a large degree, the American Holiness Movement. So, New York City honored the memory of this native daughter.

Phoebe Palmer

Phoebe's father was Henry Worrall, a native of Yorkshire, England. At 14, Henry would rise to go hear John Wesley preach. He joined a Methodist society and received his first membership ticket from Wesley's own hand. He sailed to America when he was about 25, settled in New York City, and married.

The Worralls had nine children who survived childhood. Sarah and Phoebe were born in 1806 and 1807 respectively. Phoebe married Dr. Walter C. Palmer, a physician whose father was a longtime Methodist class leader. Sarah married Thomas Lankford, an architect. New York City was one of the hubs of American Methodism, and the extended Worrall family became one of the leading families in New York City Methodism.

The first years of Walter and Phoebe Palmer's marriage were marred by tragedy. Phoebe gave birth twice. Twice, the child died soon after birth. Their large house was still relatively empty, and so when Sarah and Thomas Lankford married in 1831, the Palmers invited the newlyweds to share the house with them. The arrangement lasted nearly ten years. Like physicians of the day, Walter Palmer had his office in the house and saw patients there. In time, Phoebe gave birth to four other children. One of these also died, but three survived infancy and reached adulthood.

The two sisters devoted themselves to church causes. They led Bible classes for young women, participated in missionary promotion, and did charity work.

Sarah Lankford also led weekly prayer meetings for women at two different Methodist churches. In 1835, she persuaded the two groups to combine, and their meeting was held thereafter in the Palmer-Lankford home every Tuesday afternoon. The Tuesday Meeting became so successful that men asked for the privilege of accompanying their wives. In 1839, the women consented and agreed to admit the men.

Phoebe Palmer's activity was not limited to participating in the Tuesday Meeting. She began a Bible class for young women at Allen Street M. E. Church that grew to nearly 60 members. Her husband was a Methodist class leader at this time, but as his medical practice grew, he was sometimes absent. By 1839, Phoebe was in the habit of leading this class in his absence.

In December 1839, Palmer was appointed to head her own Methodist class of men and women—the first time a woman had been appointed to such a position in New York City. It is not so clear whether she was the first woman to head a mixed class of men and women in American Methodism, but one thing *is* clear: her success in this hub of northern Methodism led to the appointment of women as class leaders on a wider scale.

The Lankfords moved to another city in 1840, and Palmer assumed leadership of the Tuesday Meeting for the Promotion of Holiness. Since those in attendance were not in need of evangelism but of Christian nurture, the emphasis was on developing Christian lives that reflected conformity to Christ's example. Phoebe Palmer's personal rediscovery of John Wesley's emphasis on Christian perfection became the cornerstone of her ever-enlarging ministry.

Once the Tuesday Meeting was opened to men, it attracted some of the notable leaders of the day. Thomas Upham, a noted New England philosopher, became a regular while spending a few months in New York to write a book. Other notables included Nathan Bangs, one of the most pre-eminent Methodists of the 19th century, who headed the Methodist Book Concern; nearly a dozen bishops, most notably Bishops Hamline and Janes; John Dempster, founder of both Boston University's School of Theology and Garrett Biblical Seminary; and Stephen Olin, later president of Drew University.

Phoebe Palmer's able leadership of the class meeting and the Tuesday Meeting brought invitations in the summer of 1840 to speak in

other cities. This was the beginning of her ministry from the platform. Her early trips to Philadelphia and Jersey City were followed by an ever-widening circle of cities that took her to Maryland and Massachusetts, and then to Canada. At each city, she spoke to largely Methodist gatherings interested in the recovery of the emphasis on Christian perfection.

Palmer's first book was *The Way of Holiness,* published in 1843. Other books followed. She wrote numerous articles for the New York *Christian Advocate,* a Methodist paper. In the 1850s, she became a popular speaker at Methodist camp meetings. Walter Palmer was drawn into his wife's travels so fully that he eventually abandoned his medical practice and became a lay revivalist as well. Meanwhile, the Tuesday Meeting for the Promotion of Holiness became widely imitated throughout American Methodism.

The Palmers played an important role in the Laymen's Revival, which broke out in various Eastern cities in 1857 and 1858. The revival, directed by lay people, not clergy, was characterized by businessmen and women gathering for noontime prayer services.

In 1859, the Palmers accepted an invitation to visit Great Britain. For the next four years, they labored in England, Ireland, Scotland, and Wales, often attracting audiences of thousands.

Upon returning to America, Walter Palmer purchased a Holiness paper named *The Guide to Christian Perfection.* Phoebe became its editor and changed its name to *The Guide to Holiness.* Its circulation multiplied four-fold and grew to over 40,000 by the time she died.

She also continued writing books. *Promise of the Father,* published in 1859 to defend women's right to preach the gospel in the dispensation of the Holy Spirit, was one of her lengthier books. So, too, was *Four Years in the Old World*, an account of the Palmers' travels abroad.

After Phoebe Palmer died in 1874, Methodist minister Asbury Lowry wrote: "Her license came from no subordinate source. She was accredited from on high. Her authority and credentials were conferred by the Holy Ghost. She was set apart and gifted to be a gentle leader."

### B. T. Roberts
### *The Impulse of a Free Methodist*

The schism that led Free Methodists out of the Methodist Episcopal Church in 1860 crystallized around social issues that still resonated when the Nazarene parent bodies originated in the 1880s and 90s.

B. T. Roberts

Opposition to slavery was a critical element in Free Methodism's rise. The slavery issue troubled the Methodist Episcopal Church from its beginning in 1784. In 1843, Wesleyan Methodists left because the M. E. Church had not condemned slavery and did not appear likely to do so. In 1844, the M. E. Church itself divided—one church for the North, the other for the South. Still the northern church's General Conference refused to condemn slavery, fearing that annual conferences in the border states would unite with "the Church South" if they did so. Abolitionist sentiments, heightened by perfectionist tendencies, fired the hearts of Free Methodists in 1860.

Nevertheless, there were other issues behind Free Methodism's rise, many spelled out by the church's principal founder, Benjamin Titus Roberts, in his article, "New School Methodism" (1857); his book, *Why We Need Another Sect* (1879); and his paper, *The Earnest Christian*.

Roberts was a Methodist minister in the Genesee Conference of New York when he first decried the growing worldliness in the church. He attacked lodge memberships by Methodist clergy and laity, especially the Masons and Odd Fellows. He had various objections. For one thing, secret societies bred a "brotherhood" mentality among its members, but that "brotherhood" was restrictive—it was not open to all, but only to "the right kind" of people. Further, fraternal ties competed with the Christian ministry's own brotherhood ideal, dividing the ministers into two groups when they should be united by their ordination vows. Roberts had evidence that the stationing of ministers was affected by lodge ties, not a congregation's needs and a given minister's ability to meet them. A church whose key members belonged to a certain lodge might insist that a minister be appointed who shared their fraternal association. The ideal at the heart of Methodism's appointive system of ministry was being defeated. In his struggle with the conference over the issue, Roberts ironically received support from "some well known Masons, both in the Conference and out of it," who "insisted that it was a gross perversion of Masonry to use it as a means for controlling the affairs of a church." The Free Methodist Church, when it was organized, banned membership in secret societies.

Another issue behind the schism concerned the poor. Fashionable Methodist churches in the East rented pews to its wealthier members to help retire church debts. Those who could not afford a rented pew sat in less desirable parts of the sanctuary. Roberts objected that rich and poor were treated differently, and that this was neither true Christianity nor true Methodism. By contrast, the Free Methodist Discipline required that

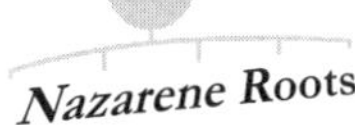

all pews be free. The "Free" in Free Methodist stood, then, for free blacks, free pews, and freedom from secret societies.

The Church of the Nazarene arose after the slavery issue was settled by a bloody Civil War, and it reconciled people alienated from one another by the sectional tensions generated by slavery and war. Nazarenes shared Free Methodism's concern for the poor, and pew rentals were contrary to the ideals of Nazarene founders. B. T. Roberts' well-publicized struggle against secret societies had a direct influence on Nazarenes. His stand, reflected in Bresee's *Manual* of 1905 and the Holiness Church of Christ's *Manual* of 1904, was incorporated into the 1908 *Manual* of the united church.

## John Inskip
### *First President of the National Holiness Association*

John Inskip

The Civil War was still fresh in the minds of Americans when the first "National Camp Meeting for the Promotion of Holiness" convened at Vineland, New Jersey, in 1867. It featured 26 preachers and lasted from July 17 to 26. Over 10,000 people attended on the Sunday that Bishop Matthew Simpson preached, and organizers concluded that a permanent organization should be established to foster annual camp meetings of this type throughout the United States.

And so, the National Camp Meeting Association for the Promotion of Holiness was organized, and John Inskip was elected as its first president.

Inskip was born in Huntingdon, England, in 1816. His family migrated to America when he was five and settled in Pennsylvania. He was converted to Christ at age 16 under the ministry of Levi Scott, later a Methodist bishop. Inskip entered the Methodist ministry when he was 19.

His presiding elders and bishops quickly noted Inskip's superior abilities in preaching and pastoral care. After he gained experience, he became a highly mobile pastor whose appointment to churches in a variety of different annual conferences was very unusual in the Methodist system. He became the pastor of large churches in several major urban areas, including Philadelphia, Cincinnati, New York City, and Baltimore.

Inskip was an innovator, and this was one secret to his success. His innovations did not always meet with approval, at least initially. He encouraged families at his congregation in Springfield, Ohio, to sit

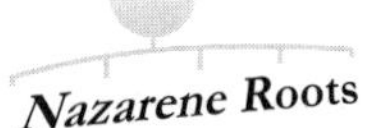


together during church services. It was customary in American churches for the men to sit on one side of the sanctuary, while women sat together on the other side. So, Inskip's action shocked many ministers and laity of his day, who regarded this "promiscuous seating" as "a prostitution of the house of God." He was actually brought to church trial for this, and found guilty. But he appealed the verdict to the General Conference of the Methodist Church, which exonerated him. His innovation was standard practice within a few years.

Inskip was a successful camp meeting revivalist at the time the National Camp Meeting Association was born. But the association he led was breaking new ground in two ways. First, American camp meetings had focused on converting sinners and bringing them to grace, but the National Holiness Association (as it was nick-named) focused on bringing those who already were Christians into the grace of perfect love. There were, indeed, conversions. Bishop Simpson's son was converted at the first National Camp Meeting. Still, the focus of these camps lay elsewhere—on entire sanctification.

The National Holiness Association also broke new ground by planning camp meetings in different locations. Prior to this, camp meetings were local affairs under the aegis of local boards. The NHA sponsored holiness camp meetings in different states, often near urban areas, by renting local camp meeting grounds and advertising the meeting nationally. It was not unusual to attract participants from many states and even from other nations.

Holiness Greats at Camp Meeting

Inskip played a key role in organizing the second national camp meeting in 1868, conducted at Manheim, Pennsylvania. The "majestic forest" surrounding the camp grounds was the setting where nearly 25,000 gathered on the camp's final Sunday. In 1870, national camp meetings were conducted in three states. In 1871, the organization shifted its attention west, holding camp meetings in Salt Lake City, Sacramento, San Francisco, and Santa Clara, and yet other camp meetings in Indiana, New York, and Ohio.

The growing success of the holiness camp meeting movement led Inskip to consult with his bishop, and, in 1871, he stepped aside from pastoral ministry. With the bishop's approval, Inskip became a full-time holiness evangelist. He worked closely for the rest of his career with

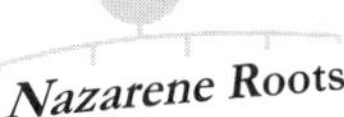


William McDonald, who succeeded him as president of the NHA in 1884.

In 1880, John and Martha Inskip embarked on a world tour to conduct holiness revivals in other countries. In keeping with the NHA's philosophy of bringing believers into a "higher state of grace," they targeted countries where Methodism had already made an impact, especially India and Australia.

Douglas Camp Meeting, cottage owned by the People's Pentecostal Church

The Inskips were not alone for the first part of the tour. William McDonald, John A. Wood, and their wives accompanied them. The group carried a large revival tent. They stayed in England for three months, where they conducted nearly 200 services before going on to India.

In India, they connected with William B. Osborne, who had helped plan the first National Camp Meeting and now was a presiding elder (district superintendent) in the South India Conference. Osborne happily told his friends that "most, if not all, of the preachers of the South India Conference were earnest in their advocacy of holiness." They rejoiced, at one service, when all the preachers of the conference "were on their knees at the altar, seeking the fullness of God."

After several months conducting holiness revivals in India, the evangelistic group broke up. The McDonalds and Woods returned to America via Europe, while John and Martha Inskip sailed east to conduct holiness meetings in Australia. Again they renewed acquaintances with old friends and ministered there for two months. Inskip preached an average of 10 times a week while in Australia. By the time they arrived back home, they had conducted over 500 services.

Inskip edited the *Christian Standard and Home Journal* throughout the latter part of his career. Even the world tour did not prevent him from reaching out to the paper's readers. He wrote over 160 editorials for the *Christian Standard* while abroad, informing readers about the churches and cultures he witnessed in other parts of the world.

John Inskip's health suffered from the weariness and stress of the world tour. Friends remarked that he was never quite the same afterward. In 1884—two years after returning to America—he died at his home near the Methodist camp ground in Ocean Grove, New Jersey.

Inskip's legacy was carried on by many others. The National Holiness Association adapted to changing circumstances and became the Christian

Holiness Association. It was the first and longest-lived Wesleyan-Holiness association in America.

## German Methodism
### *The Influence of Ethnic Religious Communities*

The core of the early Nazarene movement was composed of dissenters from Episcopal Methodism, leavened by those from other religious traditions, including some Quakers, Presbyterians, and Baptists. "German Methodism" was one of the traditions that leavened the Nazarene loaf.

"We are brothers!"

German Methodism embraced three separate groups: the Church of the United Brethren in Christ, the Evangelical Association (known after 1922 as the Evangelical Church), and the German conferences of the Methodist Episcopal Church.

The latter were ethnic enclaves in mainstream Methodism that used the German language in preaching and periodicals. They were stronger in northern Methodism than in the South, since German Americans generally held anti-slavery views. William Nast (1807-89), editor, revivalist, and missionary to Germany, was the outstanding leader in German Conference work within the Methodist Church. Nast's biographer states: "To him, sanctification was a fact and not a theory; it could be experienced and demonstrated." Nast joined the National Holiness Association and was welcomed by its leaders as one of their own, even though he smoked a pipe (this was excused as an ethnic trait). His portrait graced a poster of Holiness "greats" issued at the General Holiness Assembly of 1901.

The two other branches of German Methodism were completely independent of the Methodist church, yet had amazing affinity with it. Why? The answer lies in the common heritage of European pietism, a Protestant movement in the 17th and 18th centuries that crossed denominational lines. Pietism stressed a personal relationship to God, with an identifiable conversion experience; sanctification or the holy life; and the witness of the Spirit. Methodism resulted from Pietism's impact on Anglicanism (or the Church of England) through John Wesley's relationship with the Moravians, a German Pietist sect. The United Brethren sprang from Pietism's impact on Reformed (Calvinist) and Mennonite communities; the Evangelical Association was a product of Lutheran pietism.

With different theological traditions in their backgrounds, what brought Evangelicals and United Brethren under the broad umbrella of "German

Methodism"? Pietism provided a common religious vocabulary, centered on the warmed heart that United Brethren, Evangelicals, and Methodists shared, and which Nazarenes and other Holiness churches perpetuate today. Common religious experiences and vocabulary promoted bonds of theological and social fraternity between Methodism and the two German sects—so close, in fact, that by 1968, all three were joined into a single denomination: the United Methodist Church.

Philip William Otterbein

The United Brethren in Christ were formed by Philip William Otterbein (1726-1813), a German Reformed minister, and Martin Boehm (1725-1812), a Mennonite bishop. Otterbein was born in Germany and educated for the ministry. He immigrated to the American colonies in 1752, becoming pastor of the Reformed Church in Lancaster, PA. After seeking and finding the assurance of faith in 1752, Otterbein gave the concerns of Pietism increasing emphasis, joining with other Reformed ministers and laity in 1774 to establish a band of seekers after holiness.

In 1767, Otterbein attended the preaching of Martin Boehm in a barn in Lancaster County, PA. After hearing a warm sermon on salvation, Otterbein took Boehm's hand and said: *"Wir sind brüder* (We are brothers)." Their common interest on the warmed heart cut across denominational boundaries, and in 1800, the men and their followers organized the Church of the United Brethren in Christ.

Martin Boehm

Close relations existed with the Methodists. Otterbein laid hands on Francis Asbury, father of American Methodism, at the latter's consecration as bishop, while Boehm belonged to a Methodist class meeting and helped organize a church of that denomination on family land. His son, Henry, became Francis Asbury's traveling companion and a Methodist preacher. Many Methodist features (all familiar to Nazarenes) soon characterized the United Brethren: a quadrennial general meeting, an episcopacy understood as a general superintendency, equal representation by laity and elders at delegated meetings, mode of baptism left to the conscience of the candidate, and a missionary emphasis.

The Evangelical Association, the third branch of German Methodism, was founded by Jacob Albright (1759-1808). A son of German immigrants to Pennsylvania, Albright was educated in a Lutheran school. He was a drummer in the militia when the American Revolution began in 1776 and later became an army regular. He married, bought a farm, and started a business manufacturing roof tiles. He came into contact with followers of William Otterbein and was influenced by their brand of German pietism. After three of his children died during an epidemic in 1790, Albright sought and found a deeper experience of faith. He joined a Methodist class meeting and was licensed to preach.

Jacob Albright

Albright began a wider itinerant ministry in 1796, preaching in homes and schoolhouses to German folk throughout Pennsylvania, Maryland, and Virginia. In true Methodist style, he organized followers into classes; and in 1807, the classes formally organized as a new religious body whose German name meant "The Newly-Formed Methodist Conference." It was not a part of the Methodist Church, however, but a separate organization. Albright was elected bishop, but died the next year, and in 1816, the group adopted the name Evangelische Gemeinschaft, or Evangelical Association. Its *Discipline,* or church manual, was patterned after that of the Methodist Episcopal Church.

Committed to Wesleyan revivalism and doctrine, Evangelical itinerant preachers moved ever westward, organizing new churches wherever German immigrants settled. In 1853, the church headquarters were moved to Cleveland, Ohio, indicative that the denomination's geographical center of gravity had shifted. By 1880, the English language was used in nearly half of the Association's churches. In 1922, the name was changed to the Evangelical Church, and in 1946, it united with Otterbein's United Brethren, creating the Evangelical United Brethren Church. In 1968, EUBs and Methodists joined to form the United Methodist Church.

While most early Nazarene leaders traced their spiritual lineage to the main branches of American Methodism, some had spiritual and doctrinal roots in German Methodism. C. W. Ruth and Jonas Trumbaur, nurtured in the Evangelical Association, became leaders in the Holiness Christian Church, which began as an evangelistic society founded primarily by Evangelical clergy and laity. It evolved into a separate denomination. Horace Trumbaur, son of Jonas, led the Pennsylvania Conference of the HCC into the Pentecostal Church of the Nazarene in 1908. Ruth had already united earlier with Bresee's Nazarene movement in Los Angeles, becoming assistant general superintendent, and was the major broker in the series of denominational marriages of 1907 and 1908 to which we trace our present church. Ruth was one of the most influential revivalists in the holiness movement of his day, and his writings reflect the deep imprint of German Pietism on his spirituality, his theological vocabulary, and his basic conception of Christianity.

H. Orton Wiley was another product of German Methodism. Raised in the United Brethren Church, Wiley was sanctified under C. W. Ruth's ministry in 1902 and licensed to preach later that year. He served a UB

circuit of churches until uniting with the Nazarenes in 1905. Wiley became the premier Nazarene theologian of his day, acknowledged outside Wesleyan circles as a major representative of Arminian theology.

C. W. Ruth and Horace Trumbaur

The Ludwig family came from the St. Louis German Conference of the Methodist Episcopal Church. Theodore and Minnie Ludwig became highly regarded Nazarene revivalists. Son of an immigrant, Theo was converted at Salem (German) Methodist Church, which stood on his father's Illinois farm. Trained at Garrett, he pastored German Conference M.E. churches for thirteen years. He was ordained by Bishop Stephen Merrill, a holiness exponent, while his wife was later ordained by Dr. Bresee. They and their son, S. T., became Nazarenes in 1912. Theo Ludwig served as chairman of the General Orphanage Board and district superintendent, while S. T. Ludwig was a college president and, from 1944-64, general church secretary. He was succeeded by another product of German Methodism, B. Edgar Johnson. Raised in the Evangelical Church, Johnson pastored in that denomination until becoming a Nazarene. He was general secretary from 1964-90.

What should the heritage of German Methodism mean to us?

First, it underscores the vitality of ethnic ministries.

Second, those who entered the Church of the Nazarene from German Methodism have reinforced the Wesleyan and pietist roots of our denominational identity, enriching the whole.

## Sam Jones
### *Southern Evangelist*

Samuel Porter Jones

Sam Jones was not identified with the Holiness Movement directly, yet he influenced a generation of southern Holiness preachers. A Georgia Methodist, Jones was far better known to southern folk than his contemporary, D. L. Moody. Jones inspired dozens of imitators and was an ally of the Holiness preachers during the "evangelist controversy" that broke out in southern Methodism in the 1890s. His case proved a watershed for the southern Holiness Movement.

Samuel Porter Jones was born in Alabama in 1847. His mother died when he was eight. Sam's father remarried, moving the family to Cartersville, Georgia. By the time he married, Jones was an alcoholic. He was admitted to the Georgia bar, but his law practice disintegrated due to his addiction. The turning point came at his father's death. Jones became receptive to the guidance of his grandfather, a sanctified Methodist preacher. He was converted and entered the ministry, pastoring Methodist churches from 1872 to 1880. From 1880 to 1892, he was the agent for the North Georgia Conference Orphan's Home.

His evangelistic ministry began in 1883, while raising funds for the Orphan's Home. Jones conducted a two-week revival for the Methodist churches of Louisville. The next year, he held a city-wide revival in Memphis sponsored by ministers from five denominations. Revivals in other cities quickly followed, including one in DeWitt Talmage's Brooklyn church. Jones' Nashville revival in 1885 attacked political corruption and appealed to civic and moral reform. Crowds packed every session as Jones preached three times daily for four weeks. The Nashville press called him "the Moody of the South." Others called him the most popular American preacher after Moody and Talmage. Before he died, Jones held revivals in every major American city.

His ministry challenged the practice of the M.E. Church, South. The Southern Methodist *Discipline* did not allow full-time evangelists. Each pastor was to be a revivalist, and neighboring pastors held meetings for one another. This was a time-honored principle. In 1892, Bishop Haygood appointed Jones to a church, but Jones turned the charge over to an assistant and resumed his itinerary. The stage was set for a confrontation. At the 1893 North Georgia Annual Conference, Haygood forced Jones to accept the pastoral appointment or revert to the status of a lay preacher. Jones chose the latter. The 1894 General Conference heard his appeal but sustained the bishop. Under his new status as a local preacher, Jones pursued his evangelistic ministry until death in 1906.

A sizable group of lesser-known evangelists had sprung up in every conference of the M. E. Church, South. Some were Holiness evangelists; others were not. The 1894 General Conference in Memphis threw down a gauntlet. A section in the Episcopal Address on "Modern Evangelists" deplored their evasion of church law for refusing to submit to the appointive ministry.

As Jones' case moved through the church system, so did that of Robert Lee Harris in the Memphis Conference. However, Harris withdrew in 1894 and began the first Nazarene parent-body in the South. In 1899, a separate colony of Holiness evangelists led by E. C. DeJernett formed near Greenville, Texas. In 1903, another colony of former Methodist evangelists had gathered at nearby Pilot Point. Around "the evangelist controversy," the foundations of the Church of the Nazarene in the South were laid.

**William Taylor**
***The World-Wide Missionary***

The 19th-century Holiness Movement had risk-takers, and few excelled William Taylor, whose entrepreneurial approach to missions inspired scores of others to follow him to distant lands. Born in Virginia in 1821, he was about 10 when his father was converted in a camp meeting and became a Methodist preacher. Taylor's conversion occurred at 20. He, too, entered the ministry.

William Taylor

Taylor became a home mission pastor in San Francisco in 1849. The ship's journey around South America initiated an excitement-filled seven-year pastorate. In San Francisco, Taylor constructed a house for family, and then he set out to plant Methodism as one of only two Methodist preachers in the state. Taylor preached to Chinese immigrants, sailors, and gold seekers. He built a church building, later adding a book room and temperance boardinghouse, in a rough-and-tumble culture.

Disaster struck in year seven. The boardinghouse burned. Taylor had borrowed money for it and was responsible for the debt. He left pastoral work, returned east, and entered full-time evangelism. To pay his debts, he wrote books about his California adventures. A capable evangelist, his itinerary rarely lagged. In Canada, he learned that preachers were needed in Australia, so in 1863 his family sailed there. He preached in Australia and New Zealand for three years. He supported his family through writings and used the money raised in revivals to build chapels. He was invited to preach in other sectors of the British Empire, and Taylor preached for three years in South Africa, the West Indies, and England.

Taylor's world was completely changed by 1870. The missionary spirit displayed in California had moved to a wider canvas. His career was now devoted to missionary work on three continents, punctuated by visits to America and England to raise money and recruit workers. India absorbed his attention from 1870 to 1875. The South American continent did the same from 1875 to 1884. Planting missions in Africa occupied him from 1884 to 1896.

Taylor articulated a philosophy called Pauline missions. His goal was to develop national churches as quickly as possible. He considered traditional mission agencies as patronizing. He established churches, not missions, in India. The church buildings looked Indian, not European, in style. He argued that missionaries should be self-supporting—either bi-vocational or by working in teams in which the labor of some team members financed the entire team, leaving others to evangelize. He recruited faith missionaries who shared this vision, and he inspired imitators. The American Holiness Movement, itself at odds with institutional methods, gave Taylor moral and financial support.

His methods conflicted with American and British Methodists already in India. Was Taylor's network part of the Methodist Church or not? A compromise was reached. Taylor put his network under the Methodist mission board's authority but remained its superintendent. It developed into the South India Conference of the Methodist Episcopal Church.

Taylor was invited to South America, where he created another church network independent of mission boards. One strategy was to sign contracts to provide teachers for schools in Chile. Then he recruited teacher-missionaries to fulfill the contract. Some recruits died of tropical diseases; others were disillusioned. Many others succeeded. Taylor's relationship to the Methodist Episcopal Church was again scrutinized. In 1882 the denomination again sought to bring his missions under their guidance.

In the midst of the controversy, Taylor was elected as the Methodist Episcopal Church's first bishop for Africa! It was a stunning reversal of fortunes for a maverick, and it was due to the organized efforts of Holiness movement leaders. He was 63, and this new challenge dominated his remaining career. Taylor envisioned churches stretching across Africa, east to west, and set to work building it. He labored until forced to retire at 75. His last days were spent in California, where he died in 1902.

The denominational boards that Taylor spurned saved phases of his work from collapsing, while his bracing vision spurred a more rapid growth of churches. His passion for missions rallied many to the cause, creating interest that benefited Taylor and his critics alike.

# Chapter 3

# *Spirit of the Founders*

## Introduction

The founders shaped the Church of the Nazarene's initial trajectory. Their vision brought the church into existence, their energies propelled it forward for a generation, and their values were enshrined in its doctrine and structures. But is their vision still relevant to our time and culture? To answer that, we must ask questions: What did the founders intend? What were their principal concerns? What methods did they use?

Their fundamental purpose was to attain unity in holiness. To achieve this, they promoted the religion of the heart by emphasizing Christian conversion, the sanctification of believers, including their entire sanctification, and faithful discipleship. To support this fundamental purpose, they also believed that the Church of the Nazarene should preserve an apostolic ministry inclusive of women, be in active ministry to the poor, and be committed to carrying out a mission to the world. They agreed that these aims were best accomplished through a structure adapted from Methodism that had been democratized and reformed.

The founders differed widely in temperament and abilities. Phineas Bresee was noted for the power of his preaching and his dignity. He inspired confidence in his ideas, whether theological or organizational. He endowed the Church of the Nazarene with a specific frame of government adapted from the Methodist Episcopal Church, in which he labored for over 35 years. Hiram F. Reynolds was noted for his passion for world evangelization and his great endurance as the most widely traveled of all the founders. He helped stamp the church with its missionary character and laid the foundations for its international development. William Howard Hoople was not known as a great preacher, but *he was known as a great pastor*. His enthusiasm never failed to rally the people, and he lifted his melodious voice in song whenever the worship service lagged, raising the spirits of his congregation. C. W. Ruth was a national Holiness evangelist whose vision for uniting the different Holiness groups was born out of his wide personal travels and contacts. C. B. Jernigan began his Nazarene years as a bi-vocational district superintendent with five churches on his Oklahoma-Kansas District. For the first year, he traveled the district with a tent, used his camera to take people's portraits during the day, and preached revival services at night. He organized a church if there was sufficient interest. His passion for church planting and rugged determination quickly gave Oklahoma a larger concentration of Nazarenes than any state except California. Mary Lee Cagle planted over 20 churches. Behind the pulpit, she had a dignified bearing and "preached with tears." She inspired dozens of women to enter the Nazarene ministry. George Sharpe entered the Methodist ministry in America but returned to his native Scotland, where his unswerving commitment to the Wesleyan-Holiness message gave rise to a new Scottish denomination that merged with the Nazarenes in 1915. He gave strong support to the pioneer medical ministries of his daughter and son-in-law, Kanema and David Hynd, in Swaziland.

The founders had various strengths, but all were committed to establishing a denomination in the Wesleyan-Holiness tradition. Every Nazarene generation since then has stood on their shoulders.

**Fred Hillery**
***New England Roots***

On March 13-14, 1890, representatives from several churches and local Holiness associations in southern New England met at Rock, MA. They agreed upon some basic principles, pledged themselves "to promote scriptural holiness by united and concerted action," and thereupon launched the Central Evangelical Holiness Association as a regional organization. Of the seven parent bodies that pre-dated the Pentecostal Church of the Nazarene of 1908, the Central Evangelical Holiness Association arrived first on the scene. It preceded by over five years all but one of the others.

The leading lights of the New England organization included two of its original officers: Fred A. Hillery, vice president; and C. Howard David, secretary. Hillery's story illustrates the spirit that motivated the New England Holiness Movement.

Fred A. Hillery

A printer by trade, Hillery was Sunday School superintendent in St. Paul's Methodist Episcopal Church of South Providence, RI, when a struggle ensued in the congregation over the doctrine and nature of entire sanctification. Hillery and others eventually withdrew. In July 1887, they organized the People's Evangelical Church with 51 members. The church was incorporated the following year. Hillery was the congregation's spiritual shepherd from the beginning, and, in 1889, he was ordained to the ministry in an impressive service conducted by 13 independent Holiness ministers from around New England. He remained pastor of the People's Church until 1904.

The 1895 *Manual* of the People's Church shows that it observed a strict rule designed to create a disciplined and faithful community. Among the grounds for admonition and church discipline were "neglecting family prayers" and "unnecessary absence from class or communion." Primary concerns were reflected in the church's administrative structure, which had five committees: Sunday School, the Sick and Destitute, Care of the Church, Finance, and Baptism.

The various *Manuals* and *Disciplines* of other churches in the Central Evangelical Holiness Association show that they, too, were committed to a style of churchmanship that emphasized an integral relationship between the "visible church" and Christian ethics and spirituality. Among those congregations were: the Bethany Mission Church (Keene, NH), the Mission Church (Lynn, MA), the People's Mission Church (Central Falls, RI), the Independent Congregational Church (Rock, MA), the Emanuel Mission Church (North Attleboro, MA), and others.

In 1888, Fred Hillery was founding editor of *Beulah Items*, a paper published on behalf of the People's Evangelical Church. By 1892, when its name changed to the *Beulah Christian*, the paper reported on happenings throughout the Central Evangelical Holiness Association.

In 1896-97, a merger united the bulk of the Central Evangelical Holiness Association with the Association of Pentecostal Churches of America, the latter begun in 1895 under the leadership of William Howard Hoople of Brooklyn, NY. The name of the newer body was retained as that of the unified body. Hillery's *Beulah Christian* became the APCA's official organ. Later, from 1907-11, it was an official paper of the Pentecostal Church of the Nazarene, serving the constituency in the eastern United States. Hillery published it until 1915.

### William Howard Hoople
### *The Association of Pentecostal Churches of America*

William H. Hoople

To *Christian Witness* readers, William Howard Hoople described himself, in 1895, as a Congregationalist who had "embraced Methodist doctrine," and this logic lay behind the churches he shepherded in Brooklyn, NY. He rejected American Methodism's episcopal system, but, as an adherent of "Methodist doctrine," was unwelcome in the Calvinistic church that nurtured his early faith in Christ.

Hoople was born in Herkimer, NY, in 1868 to Canadian immigrants. They moved to Brooklyn shortly thereafter. His father, a wealthy leather merchant, exerted a Christian influence, and Hoople was converted as a young man. He followed his father into business and prospered. He married Victoria Crawford in 1891. They had a daughter and five sons.

His conversion to "Methodist doctrine" occurred after he began attending a prayer meeting at John Street Methodist Church in Manhattan. There, he met Charles BeVier, choir director at a large Methodist church in Brooklyn and an ardent exponent of Wesleyan-Holiness experience. Hoople soon testified to his own experience of sanctifying grace and joined forces with BeVier to open a mission to the poor at 123 Schenectady Avenue on January 4, 1894.

By June, it was a full-fledged church of 37 members with Hoople as its pastor. A sanctuary "in a new and rapidly developing part of the city" was dedicated on June 15. The participation of the Rev. D. V. Gwillym, "the High Church" rector of a nearby Episcopal congregation, signaled community favor.

The Utica Avenue Church was but the first in a new denomination that Hoople and BeVier fostered. Other churches soon appeared in the city. Hoople, ordained in late 1894, planted Bedford Avenue Pentecostal Church in east Brooklyn in early 1895. John Norberry became its pastor. The Emmanuel Pentecostal Tabernacle soon followed, organized on Labor Day.

In December, church representatives organized the Association of Pentecostal Churches of America. The name reflected a national vision at the outset, and through merger and aggressive evangelism, the denomination stretched from Nova Scotia to Iowa within a decade.

A church was organized in Cliftondale, NY, in mid-1896 after a camp meeting revival. H. F. Reynolds, a visiting Methodist from Vermont, decided to unite with the small denomination during that revival; he claimed that God had clearly called him to do so. Susan Fitkin, A. B. Riggs, H. N. Brown, and other New England Holiness stalwarts soon did the same. Reynolds brought solid experience as a pastor and evangelist—and connections throughout the Holiness Movement in the Northeast. Meanwhile, BeVier organized the John Wesley Pentecostal Church in Brooklyn in October. He was ordained and called as its first pastor.

William H. Hoople and John Norberry

Reynolds was only one factor in the union of the APCA and a New England denomination, the Central Evangelical Holiness Association founded in 1890. Another was the *Christian Witness* of Boston, which published frequent reports from churches and ministers in both groups. Long before Hoople met his New England counterparts, they had read of each other's work.

The groundwork of union was laid in November when Fred Hillery (Providence, RI), C. Howard Davis (Lynn, MA), and other New England pastors met with leaders of the New York movement in Hoople's parlor. A plan of union was approved after two days of discussion. The Association of Pentecostal Churches of America's name better reflected their common purpose and became that of the united body. A snag developed: several New England churches refused to enter the union. Most CEHA churches united anyway. Hillery brought a paper, the *Beulah Christian,* into the union, and it was adopted later as the official publication.

John Norberry

The APCA grew steadily from 1897 to 1907 as churches were added in New England, the Middle Atlantic states, the District of Columbia, Canada, and the Midwest. Reynolds organized churches in Oxford and Springhill, Nova Scotia, in 1902. Others pushed the boundaries westward. A congregation in Pittsburgh led by John Norris united in 1899. By 1907, there were churches in Illinois and Iowa.

Schools and missions were the critical elements in the church program. Pentecostal Collegiate Institute, now Eastern Nazarene College, was founded in 1898. It struggled in its early years at Saratoga Springs, NY, and North Scituate, RI, finding stability only after E. E. Angell became president in 1907.

World missions were a distinctive aspect of the APCA and its primary gift to the broader Pentecostal Church of the Nazarene. Five

John C. Dias

William H. Hoople

missionaries were sent to India in 1898, the year Reynolds assumed full-time responsibility for promoting home and foreign missions. Eight others went to India in 1904 and 1905, including L. S. Tracy and Gertrude Perry, who soon married. John Dias, an immigrant from Cape Verde, was sent to his land of origin as a missionary in 1901. The administration of the missionary program was complicated by the independence of some pastors, but Reynolds' efforts were decisive in nurturing the vision of a missionary church.

The union of the Association of Pentecostal Churches of America and the Church of the Nazarene derived its initial impetus from C. W. Ruth, a National Holiness Association evangelist and the assistant general superintendent of the Church of the Nazarene. In 1906, Ruth conducted revivals in the East and was invited to an APCA meeting, where he proposed merging the two denominations. Cautious enthusiasm prevailed. Eastern pastors A. B. Riggs, John Short, and H. N. Brown—dubbed the "three wise men"—toured the Nazarene churches in the west that fall and favorably impressed Nazarene leaders.

In turn, Phineas Bresee and several associates visited the APCA's annual meeting in the spring of 1907, where the principles of merger were hammered out and union was proclaimed under the name Pentecostal

Legislative Commission at the First General Assembly, Chicago, 1907

Church of the Nazarene. The APCA brought to the union 2400 members and 45 churches, many in major eastern cities such as Pittsburg, Providence, Manchester, Saratoga Springs, Washington, and several in greater Boston, including the university city of Cambridge.

In October, the First General Assembly of the Pentecostal Church of the Nazarene met in Chicago. H. F. Reynolds was elected as the general superintendent from the east and also continued as missionary secretary for the united body. He "retired" in 1932, but carried out the tasks of a general superintendent for several more years.

Charles BeVier had died at a relatively young age in 1905, with no inkling of the outcome of his labors on behalf of the Association of Pentecostal Churches of America. The tall, genial Hoople became New York District superintendent, serving until 1911 while pastoring the John Wesley church, which grew to 350 members under his ministry. His doubts about the Pentecostal Nazarenes uniting with the southern Holiness Church of Christ evaporated at the Pilot Point General Assembly, in which he participated. Hoople became a Y.M.C.A. worker during World War I and was sent to France to provide wholesome entertainment and spiritual guidance to U. S. soldiers. His health was undermined after breathing poisonous gas. He was stationed later in Italy and Germany, and visited his daughter, a Presbyterian missionary in Peking, China, before returning to America. He died in 1922.

## Phineas F. Bresee
### *Pastor to the People*

Phineas Bresee

The intrepid Methodist circuit riders who traveled the highways and rugged trails of New York's Catskill Mountains made an indelible impression on Phineas Bresee. His ancestors had been committed Calvinists—French Huguenots who fled Catholic France for refuge in Holland. The records in the Dutch Reformed Church in Albany, New York, attest to the family's persisting loyalty to Calvinism several generations later. However in America, the family story intersected that of global Methodism and its message of free grace, empowered free will, and holy living. Some of the Bresees shifted allegiances. With no hint of irony, Phineas Bresee later referred to Methodism as the "faith of my fathers."

Bresee was born in a farmhouse on New Year's Eve in 1838. His parents were Phineas Phillips and Susan Brown Bresee. While he was still

Phineas and Maria Bresee

"The first miracle after the baptism of the Holy Ghost was wrought upon a beggar. It means that the first service of a Holy Ghost-baptized church is to the poor; that its ministry is to those who are lowest down; that its gifts are for those who need them the most. As the Spirit was upon Jesus to preach the gospel to the poor, so His Spirit is upon His servants for the same purpose."

young, they moved to a farm on the edge of West Davenport, New York. The Methodist societies ringing West Davenport maintained the religion of the "warmed heart" and provided structure to Bresee's spiritual development. At 16, he knelt at the altar rail of the Methodist church, afterward professing a personal faith in Christ. The year was 1856. Soon, he felt promptings to enter the ministry, and he received a Methodist exhorter's license.

Bresee's ministry was pursued in an arena strikingly different from New York however. In 1857, his father moved the family to Iowa, in the central United States. The mountains of New York were now far behind. The Iowa terrain was nearly all prairie. After helping his family settle, he entered the Methodist ministry as an assistant preacher. He received his own circuit of churches the next year.

The Methodist Church also provided a bride, Maria Hebbard, daughter of Horace Hebbard, a long-time Methodist class leader near Bresee's childhood home. Bresee married her in New York in the summer of 1860, then took her west to share his new life on the prairie. Four sons and three daughters were born to them.

In 1859, Bresee was ordained a deacon by Bishop Matthew Simpson. Bishop Simpson was one of the great bishops—great enough that he preached at the funeral of Abraham Lincoln in Washington, D.C., and again at Lincoln's funeral in his hometown of Springfield, Illinois. Simpson was one of Bresee's personal heroes. Two years later, after further demonstration of his worth as a pastor, Bresee was ordained an elder by Bishop Levi Scott.

Bresee's ministry grew varied. He served in rural pastorates with two- and three-point charges—the Pella and Galesburg circuits for example, which had multiple congregations under his responsibility. Then he was pastor of larger single churches in Chariton, Red Oak, and other growing communities, and in the urban centers of Des Moines and Council Bluffs. Bresee also served as a district superintendent, as a delegate to his church's General Conference, and he devoted many hours to Simpson College, one of Iowa Methodism's four schools. For many years, he served as a trustee of Simpson College; and when the school was threatened with extinction from lack of proper financing, Bresee was given the task of drawing up the plan to save the school financially, and then given the responsibility for executing his own plan. His plan was successful. The college was saved from financial ruin, and today is the leading Methodist college in Iowa.

Bresee always viewed Methodism as a revival movement. He always regarded his pastoral role as fully compatible with being a revival preacher. His involvement in the Holiness Movement, however, developed gradually over a long period of time.

After a decade of ministry, Bresee faced an increasingly difficult battle with doubt. His vocation—perhaps even his very faith—was in question. He was pastor at Chariton. Reflecting later, he stated: "My religion did not meet my needs." On a snowy winter night, after preaching a strong evangelistic message that seemed to persuade no one else, Bresee became the sole seeker at the altar. Before his own congregation, Bresee knelt, prayed, and received what he later called his "baptism with the Holy Ghost," though he admitted later that he did not know at the time *what* it was he had received.

Phineas and Maria Bresee

In 1883, Bresee moved his family to southern California. Their arrival coincided with the annual sessions of the Southern California Conference. He was introduced to a new set of clergy and was surprised to be assigned to pastor the Fort Street Church in Los Angeles, the best appointment in the conference (known today as Los Angeles First United Methodist Church). His subsequent pastorates were also in the Greater Los Angeles area. Many features of his Iowa ministry were repeated: important pastorates; service to the local Methodist college—in this case the school known today as the University of Southern California; delegate to the 1892 General Conference; and another term as district superintendent, this time of the Los Angeles District.

The "Glory Barn"

Early in Bresee's California ministry, key lay people at the Fort Street church put him in touch with the National Holiness Association. One of them was Leslie F. Gay, who introduced Bresee to key NHA figures and followed him into the Church of the Nazarene, where Gay became a noted advocate of cross-cultural missions. Bresee deepened his involvement in the National Holiness Association over the years. By the mid-1890s, he was an NHA vice-president and preached occasionally in its camp meetings and conventions in the Midwest and West.

As the Los Angeles population grew, so did the challenges of urbanization. Japanese and Chinese immigrants, brought to America as "cheap labor," mingled on the streets with Hispanics and Anglos. Bresee did not fear the ethnic diversification of Los Angeles. He regarded it as an opportunity for evangelism.

However, another aspect of urbanization bothered him greatly: a growing underclass of urban poor, trapped in cycles of despair, alcohol,

and addiction. In 1894, he requested his bishop to appoint him to be the preaching pastor at the Peniel Mission, an independent ministry in the Los Angeles slums. Since it was not sponsored by the Methodist Church, Bresee's request was unusual and was denied. Nevertheless, Bresee was convinced that God called him to this work, so he asked for a special status with the conference that placed him outside the appointive system for Methodist ministers. This was granted, and he gave his services that year to the Peniel Mission, cooperating with J. P. Widney, a leading Los Angeles physician and educator, and with the Peniel Mission founders, T. P. and Manie Ferguson.

The arrangement failed. Two strategies for reaching the poor came into conflict. The Fergusons wanted to minister primarily to transients. Bresee was convinced that the urban poor needed strong family churches in their midst to give stability to their lives and neighborhoods.

Bresee and Widney separated from the mission after a year and, with a strong core of lay people, organized an independent congregation in October 1895. At Widney's suggestion, it took the name Church of the Nazarene. Bresee and Widney were elected co-pastors and "general

The extended Bresee family in California, about 1893.
Bresee's four sons stand in the back. His parents are in the middle.

superintendents for life." Widney left the church in 1898, however, his enthusiasm for revivalism waning and his personal beliefs moving away from traditional orthodoxy.

The congregation grew steadily to nearly 1,000 members under Bresee's pastoral guidance. New churches formed in the San Francisco area in 1898. By 1905, Los Angeles had several Nazarene churches, including a Mexican congregation. The movement was spreading along the Pacific coast, and there were congregations in the Midwest, including a large one in Chicago. A substantial outreach to the Japanese immigrants in Southern California soon developed.

Phineas and Maria Bresee

Bresee's time became occupied by diverse duties. He edited the *Nazarene Messenger*, a large weekly paper. He became president of Pacific Bible College (now Point Loma Nazarene University). And he served as the full-time pastor of Los Angeles First Church until 1911.

He gave increasing attention to a union of the Holiness churches that were scattered across the United States. He relied heavily upon Rev. C. W. Ruth, his assistant general superintendent, to negotiate unions in 1907 and 1908 that brought three separate denominations into organic union as the Pentecostal Church of the Nazarene.

The first union occurred at Chicago, Illinois. Here at this First General Assembly, 50 congregations led by Bresee united with a group from the eastern United States with nearly the same number of congregations. Bresee was elected by acclamation as the first general superintendent of the united body. Later that day, H. F. Reynolds from the East was elected as his colleague.

"We want pastors who will go out and find the poor that nobody else cares for."

The next year, at Pilot Point, Texas, the Second General Assembly brought a southern group, the Holiness Church of Christ with about 75 congregations, into the union. A third general superintendent, E. P. Ellyson from Texas, joined Bresee and Reynolds on the Board of General Superintendents. This second merger constituted the Church of the Nazarene as a truly national church throughout the United States.

The graceful manner in which Bresee carried the office of general superintendent endeared him to many and played a significant role in accomplishing this union of holiness churches. J. B. Chapman, one of the southern churchmen who came into the united body at Pilot Point, reflected on the meaning of Bresee for those in the founding generation. Chapman wrote: "The first time I saw Dr. Bresee in the pulpit was when he rose to lead the devotional service on the afternoon of the opening of the 1908 General Assembly. His patriarchal appearance so impressed me that I think I was more or less prepared for the marvelous address he gave on the 60th chapter of Isaiah. . . . It was the presence and bearing and emphasis of the man that made the impression and constituted this an occasion of a lifetime—yea, even of a century. I suspect it was the climax of Dr. Bresee's life and ministry, and I suspect it was the climax of life for many of us who were there."

Bresee served as the church's senior general superintendent until his death in 1915. At the Fourth General Assembly that year, the delegates realized that he was dying and would not be with them again, so they honored him in the closing days of the assembly. In a striking ceremony, a select group of founders of the church in other parts of the United States came together around Bresee. Rev. Mary Lee Cagle presented him with a bouquet of roses, and the first general superintendent was honored as a living symbol of the ideal that had brought the Church of the Nazarene into existence: unity in holiness.

A few weeks later, Bresee died at his son's home in Los Angeles, where he had resided since leaving the Methodist ministry. The Church of the Nazarene has had other great leaders, but none has been so widely admired or cherished as Phineas F. Bresee.

Phineas Bresee at Olivet

## J. P. Widney
### *The Elusive "General Superintendent For Life"*

Over a century after he was elected "general superintendent for life" and bestowed the name "Nazarene" on our church, Joseph P. Widney of Los Angeles remains an elusive figure for many. Medical doctor and army surgeon, savant of the western desert, community leader, medical school dean, and president of the University of Southern California, Widney was a man of deep spirituality and sincere conviction.

J. P. Widney

His association with Methodist pastor Phineas F. Bresee and his role in founding the West Coast branch of our denomination is paradoxically one of the best and least known facts of his life. In later life, he consciously shied away from association with the church he named and helped to found—hurt and perhaps embittered by a painful break that resulted in Widney's withdrawal from the Church of the Nazarene in 1898. The article on Widney in the *Dictionary of American Biography* delves into his religious interests, but never mentions his Nazarene connections. Nor do numerous other articles, nor the full-length biography on Widney that Carl Rand published in 1970.

The "riddle of Widney" is a way of putting the question that admittedly occurs only from a Nazarene perspective. It arises from the unconventional course of Widney's life and the nature of his spiritual and intellectual pilgrimage. J. P. Widney was an authentic American type, a self-made man of the 19th century for whom religion was a passion and virtue a set of self-evident truths. He was a pilgrim, discontent with ever becoming a pensioner on spiritual ancestors, and his religious vision evolved through a series of spiritual-theological episodes that carried him from orthodox Methodism to the most extreme edge of liberal Christianity. His Nazarene years, in which he contributed a key element of our denominational identity—our church name—was one point on that religious continuum.

Widney's career has been described fully by his biographers. The salient facts are these: born in Ohio in 1841; migrated to California; practiced medicine in Los Angeles; founded the local medical society; was a member of the school board and the state board of health; among the founders of the University of Southern California; first dean of its medical school; and from 1892 to 1895, the college's president.

Widney became acquainted with Bresee soon after Bresee's arrival in Southern California in 1882. They became close friends later, after Bresee's election to the trustee board of U.S.C. Eventually Bresee's interest in city mission work became Widney's interest as well. Together, they became involved in the Peniel Mission in 1894, a ministry run by T. P. and Manie Ferguson. Bresee preached every Sunday between 1894-95, while Widney taught classes on the life of Jesus (the "Nazarene") and taught classes on basic nursing for inner-city workers.

They left the Peniel Mission the next year and played key roles in establishing Los Angeles First Church of the Nazarene in October 1895, the same year Widney stepped down from the presidency of U.S.C. In an early meeting of the new body, several names were proposed, most of them having the word "Methodist" in the title. Widney, however, urged the name "Church of the Nazarene," arguing that such a name stressed the new congregation's identification with Jesus' concern for "the low, toiling masses." His proposal was accepted.

Widney virtually abandoned medicine at this time, took the ministry as his second career, and became the first person ordained by Bresee at one of the earliest meetings of the Official Board of L.A. First Church. Widney and Bresee were elected joint pastors of the church and superintendents "for life."

If Widney-as-layman was a good balance for Bresee, Widney-as-clergyman was not. Different principles arose between the two, apparently propelled by changes within Widney's own viewpoint. Widney grew increasingly unhappy with the revivalistic atmosphere of the church. In 1898, he asked to start a second Nazarene congregation that he would lead. This proposal was rebuffed, and Widney left the church.

He easily negotiated the transfer of his Nazarene credentials over to the Methodist Episcopal Church, but he also insisted that he be appointed, quite irregularly, to an inner-city congregation that he was planting called the Bethel City Mission. Methodist officials usually would not have agreed to such a request, but they had a long history with him and other members of his family, all of whom had served Southern California Methodism faithfully for many years. These facts influenced their judgment, and they reluctantly agreed.

The relationship was never entirely happy, and Widney withdrew from the Methodist denomination in 1911. For the remainder of his long life, he pastored an independent congregation, the Beth-El Chapel, where he conducted services for his family and close friends.

Tragically blinded after an accident in 1929, Widney spent his last decade (the 1930s) dictating a series of books detailing his religious vision. They were published at his expense and placed in the libraries

of leading American universities. His viewpoint was strikingly different from that of his Nazarene and Methodist years. His later perspective was generally akin to that of the New England Transcendentalists. Like them, he sat lightly on the doctrines that matter most to orthodox Christians: the Trinity, the divinity of Christ, and the exclusivity of Christianity as the way of salvation. Yet unlike Emerson and Thoreau, who derived religious insight from New England's streams and wooded hills, Widney's mysticism derived from the deserts of the Southwest. Paradoxically, he remained tied to the vocabulary of the scriptural tradition.

Widney was a dissenter in the great tradition that cuts through American Christiantiy and gave rise to American religious pluralism. "The elusive Dr. Widney" was a man with a discernible impact upon our denominational consciousness, but whose spirit ultimately belonged elsewhere.

## C. B. Jernigan
### *Independent Holiness Church*

C. B. Jernigan

In 1901, the same year that C. B. Jernigan co-founded the Holiness Association of Texas, an interdenominational body, he organized the first congregation of the Independent Holiness Church, a sectarian one. Jernigan perceived no contradiction. He believed in casting wide nets.

The Southern Holiness Movement stood at a crossroads. In 1894, the Methodist Episcopal Church, South's bishops had criticized it as divisive. Itinerant evangelists, they complained, defied church polity, while proponents of the Holiness cause manifested superior attitudes. The bishops hoped, perhaps, to provide pastoral guidance; instead, their statement polarized opinion and bred confrontations. Some Holiness people had their Methodist membership revoked by pastors and church boards. Others angrily withdrew. Still others, Methodist loyalists like H. C. Morrison of Kentucky, were determined to maintain their witness within the M. E. Church, South.

Jernigan's ministry began during this struggle. Born in Mississippi during the Civil War, his family joined the post-war migration westward. He was raised in Greenville, TX, the son of a Methodist physician. He and his spouse, Johnny Hill Jernigan, became active in the Holiness Movement and were full-time revival workers by 1898.

A vision soon emerged. Increasingly, Jernigan believed that the

The Jernigan-DeJernett Evangelistic Band

scattered Holiness bands in East Texas needed to be organized into proper churches. The bands, he noted, had "no baptism, no sacraments for her people, and they were called come-outers [schismatics] by the church people." Beginning at Van Alstyne, TX, Jernigan organized receptive bands into churches and recruited pastors for them. His wider strategy was to hold the independent Holiness people of East Texas together and lead them into a wider fellowship.

He attended the General Holiness Assembly in Chicago in 1901, hoping to see a new national Holiness church organized there. He returned home disappointed. In 1902, he and his wife were ordained at Paris, TX, by Seth Rees on behalf of the Apostolic Holiness Church (later Pilgrim Holiness Church). Rees was to return in 1903 to receive Jernigan's growing number of congregations into the AHC. It did not happen. Those in the Holiness Association of Texas who disdained Jernigan's strategy persuaded Rees to abandon the effort. And in October 1904, Jernigan attended the Holiness Union in Memphis, TN, initiated by

Jernigan Family staying in the barn in Bethany

Music Group with C. B. Jernigan standing in back

H. C. Morrison, the most prominent evangelist of the southern Holiness Movement. Jernigan prayed that a southern Holiness denomination would be organized there, but Morrison, acknowledging that many wanted it, refused to lead such a move.

No wider fellowship was emerging, but Jernigan persevered in his hard-sell for organized holiness. In November 1904, he brought together representatives of the New Testament Church of Christ, the Holiness Baptists, and the Independent Holiness Church to discuss merger. The Holiness Baptists withdrew, but the others joined forces, creating the Holiness Church of Christ, with headquarters, publishing interests, and social ministries in Pilot Point, Texas.

Jernigan's quest to be part of a larger Holiness church was not yet over, but a course was now set that directly led in 1908 to the union of western, eastern, and southern Holiness churches at Pilot Point, Texas.

**Robert Lee Harris**
***The New Testament Church of Christ***

Robert Lee Harris

On July 5, 1894, Rev. Robert Lee Harris called forward those joining the New Testament Church of Christ. Thirteen came forward, and a new Holiness body was organized in Milan, Tennessee. It was the first Nazarene root organized in the South.

Robert Lee Harris was born near Okolona, Mississippi, on Christmas Day, 1861. His family soon moved to Alabama and remained there until moving to Texas when Harris was 15. He herded cattle and drifted between jobs. Though converted as a youth, he backslid, but in 1880, he was reclaimed, called to preach almost immediately, and became an itinerant evangelist. He was sanctified through the influence of Warren Parker, a Free Methodist minister in Corsicana, and entered the Free Methodist ministry in 1885. Colleagues affirmed Harris' superior gifts as a revivalist and intended to appoint him "conference evangelist." His preaching in Waco, Abilene, and other towns drew hundreds, even thousands, of listeners. District Superintendent George McCullough wrote in 1886: "There probably has not been a single minister in Texas who has been so successful in carrying forward the work of holiness."

Robert Lee Harris

Then Harris swerved from his apparent destiny and took a controversial turn. In response to an appeal for missionaries in Liberia, he volunteered and raised his own financial support. The Free Methodist founder and general superintendent, B.T. Roberts, disagreed because he opposed independent missions and considered Harris an asset to the Texas Conference. Harris also lacked a missionary's temperament. Still, he was determined, so Roberts reluctantly ordained him a deacon and elder at the General Conference of 1886. Harris stood on African soil a few weeks later.

The Liberian mission operated for four difficult years. Disease, death, and defection cut quickly into the ranks of the half-dozen workers Harris led over. Moreover, Harris' independent mission competed with the Free Methodist Church's new missions program. Discouraged by losses and growing friction with denominational leaders, Harris and two remaining workers closed the Liberian mission in early 1889. He returned to Texas, but later that year, transferred into the Methodist Episcopal Church, South, to avoid further involvement in the mission controversy and to gain a wider field of service, as he moved from one of the South's smallest denominations to one of its largest.

Lee Harris did not find the peace he sought with the southern Methodists. He did not directly enter his new denomination's ministry, but joined a congregation in Memphis as a layman and received a local preaching license. On the basis of this license, he operated as an independent evangelist outside the official system of ministerial appointments, testing church law as he did so.

In 1891, Harris married Mary Lee Wasson of Moulton, Alabama, whom he met while holding a revival. By 1894, Harris was in direct conflict with Methodist officials for scheduling revival services that competed with Methodist worship, for preaching legalistic ethics, and for organizing "Calvary holiness bands" independent of local churches and pastors. He published the *Trumpet*, an independent monthly that largely reprinted material from *The Free Methodist*. He affirmed "restorationism"—the belief (held by many Baptists) that Scripture teaches a definite form of church government that all "true churches" must follow.

Robert Lee Harris with King Tappa ca. 1890

In June 1893, the Harrises held a revival in Milan, Tennessee, where they were invited by Donie Mitchum, a sanctified Methodist Sunday School teacher. The community was receptive, and the meeting successful. Robert Balie Mitchum was a Baptist deacon, but a close friendship developed between the Mitchums and Harrises. In May 1894, a second Milan revival opened. In its midst, Lee Harris published *Why We Left the M.E. Church, South*—a critique of Methodism's episcopacy and its opposition to independent evangelists. The revival continued into the summer. Harris now had advanced tuberculosis, and three women from the Vanguard Mission in St. Louis came to assist. Two of them, Susie Sherman and Emma Woodcock, were preachers and shared the responsibility with Harris. In July, Harris organized the "church of Christ." Among its charter members were his wife; the Mitchums; Elliott J. Sheeks; and the Vanguard Mission women. Harris prepared a set of doctrines and practices, later published as *The Guidebook*, before he died in November.

Robert Lee Harris

The church did not die with its founder. Lay preachers emerged and organized congregations in Tennessee, Arkansas, and Texas. The Mitchums became the primary leaders in Tennessee. Elliott Sheeks, Ira Russell, and George Hammond led the churches in Arkansas. Mary Harris supervised the expansion in West Texas. In December 1899, Mary Harris, Elliott Sheeks, and George Hammond were ordained when the first annual council was held in Milan.

Evangelistic zeal marked the denomination. By 1904, church revivalists were holding meetings in Missouri, Alabama, Mississippi, and New Mexico, and a new general council was being contemplated when fresh contacts with the Independent Holiness Church, led by C.B. Jernigan and J.B. Chapman, led to a merger in 1904 that created the Holiness Church of Christ. Four years later, the Holiness Church of Christ merged with the Pentecostal Church of the Nazarene at Pilot Point, Texas.

**J. O. McClurkan**
***The Pentecostal Alliance***

J.O. McClurkan

"To pray well is better than to preach well, and certain are we that he who prays right will live right."

James O. McClurkan's arrival in Nashville in 1897 concluded a two-year evangelistic tour extending from California to Tennessee. It was a return to roots for him and wife, Martha Rye McClurkan. McClurkan was born in middle Tennessee in 1861. His father was a minister in the Cumberland Presbyterian Church, a denomination that sprang from the "Second Great Awakening" of the early 19th century. The church was thoroughly revivalistic in theology and practice, and McClurkan and three brothers entered its ministry.

Converted at 13, McClurkan preached his first sermon four years later at his father's urging. He studied at colleges in Tennessee and Texas and took a pastorate in 1886 in Decatur, TX. Two years later, he and Martha moved to California, serving as pastor to three churches there and a term as synod evangelist. In 1895, McClurkan attended a revival conducted by Beverly Carradine, a famous preacher in the Methodist Episcopal Church, South. McClurkan was sanctified under Carradine's preaching. Shortly afterward, he began a long trek east, conducting revivals all along the way. It took two years to return to Nashville.

Back in Tennessee, McClurkan became a natural leader of the Holiness revival there. There were others leaders, such as Methodists B.F. Haynes and Leila Owen Stratton, but McClurkan dreamed of unifying the Methodist and non-Methodist advocates of the "second blessing" into a common alliance. On July 18, 1898, the goal was accomplished when the Pentecostal Alliance opened its first convention. In time, the Alliance developed many features of a denomination, including the ordination of elders. It united many diverse elements and grew until it embraced dozens of Pentecostal missions scattered across Tennessee and into five neighboring states.

Under McClurkan's leadership, the Alliance purchased a holiness paper edited by B.F. Haynes. It was renamed *Living Water*. An ambitious

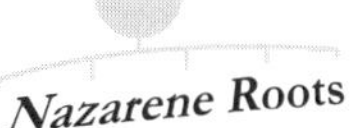


missionary program sent over 50 missionaries out before McClurkan's death in 1914. A Bible training school established early in the Alliance's life was reorganized in 1910 as Trevecca College, so named after a similar institution in early British Methodism.

McClurkan's personal affinities lay more with those in the Keswick wing of the Holiness Movement, such as A.J. Gordon and A.B. Simpson, and at one point, McClurkan entertained serious thought of uniting his work with the latter's Christian and Missionary Alliance. But the great majority of McClurkan's followers were Wesleyans like lay leader John T. Benson. After turning away from union with Simpson's group, the Alliance was renamed the Pentecostal Mission in 1902.

From 1907 on, McClurkan considered uniting his work with the Pentecostal Church of the Nazarene. Delegates from the Pentecostal Mission attended all Nazarene General Assemblies from 1908 through 1915. The 1911 General Assembly was held in Nashville specifically to woo McClurkan's body into the church, but McClurkan was suspicious of sectarianism. He believed that doctrinal statements should be broader than the essential Wesleyanism of the Nazarenes. Interdenominational work remained his ideal. He was willing for his followers to enter the Church of the Nazarene, but when they realized that he would personally hang back, they did also.

In 1914, McClurkan died at age 54. The following year, Martha Rye McClurkan and John T. Benson led the Pentecostal Mission and its ambitious missions program into the Pentecostal Church of the Nazarene. McClurkan had encouraged his wife to be a lay preacher, and the Nazarenes ordained her.

## C. W. Ruth
### *Foe of Sectarian Holiness*

C.W. Ruth

"Few men have traveled more, worked more constantly, and had more definite or larger results in their ministry than did he. His books are as clear as his preaching. His work in the National Holiness Association, both with Dr. C. J. Fowler and as leader of its 'across the nation' campaigns, was a large contribution to the total work [of the Wesleyan-Holiness movement]. He was too large to be sectarian. He loved holiness more than he loved any denomination. That was the fine evidence that he had the blessing." Such was the description of Nazarene revivalist C.

W. Ruth by a Methodist clergyman, Rev. John L. Brasher.

Ruth's opposition to narrow sectarianism was demonstrated in two aspects of his career.

The first was his tireless devotion to bringing the Church of the Nazarene into existence as a way of overcoming the plethora of small sects spawned by the American Holiness Movement. By 1900, Ruth was well aware of that movement's fragmentation.

C.W. Ruth with J.B. Chapman, 1920

Born in Pennsylvania in 1865, he was nurtured in the warm piety of the Evangelical Association, a German-American denomination of Methodist bent. He began his ministerial career in 1884 in the Holiness Christian Church, a relatively new group toward which he gravitated in his late teens. The Holiness Christian Church originated in Pennsylvania and had its centers of strength there and in Indiana. Ruth moved to Indianapolis and rose within the denomination, serving as its presiding elder for four terms.

Nevertheless, his heart lay in the area of revivalism, and in the late 1890s, he declined further leadership opportunities within his church and became an evangelist for the National Holiness Association. His field of labor became national in scope. He was regarded with great favor by the association's officers.

C.W. Ruth in 1907

Rev. C. J. Fowler, the NHA president, commended Ruth to Dr. Phineas Bresee when the latter sought Fowler's advice about a speaker to hold a revival at the Church of the Nazarene in Los Angeles. Ruth was invited to speak in the autumn of 1901 and quickly won Bresee's confidence and the people's allegiance. Within days of the meeting, Ruth was invited back to Los Angeles to assume two responsibilities: serve as the congregation's associate pastor (Bresee's first) and assume the role of assistant general superintendent. He agreed, and for the next 18 months, preached almost every Sunday evening at Los Angeles First and helped Bresee shepherd the congregation.

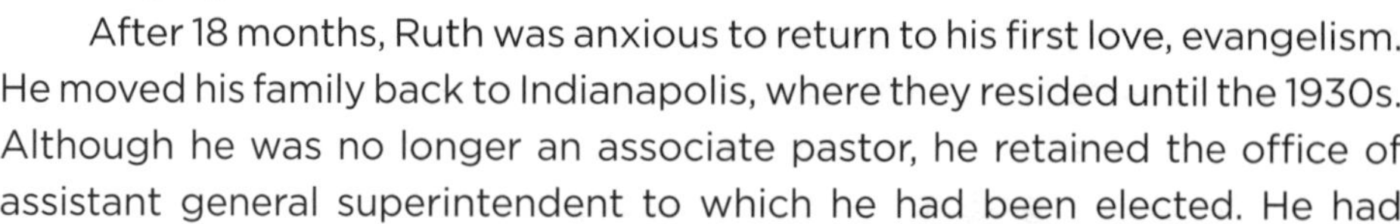

After 18 months, Ruth was anxious to return to his first love, evangelism. He moved his family back to Indianapolis, where they resided until the 1930s. Although he was no longer an associate pastor, he retained the office of assistant general superintendent to which he had been elected. He had

Bresee's blessing to exercise the responsibilities of the office as he traveled across the North American continent, conducting revival meetings in every section of the U.S. Where feasible, he organized Nazarene congregations, helping extend the small denomination beyond the West Coast where it had originated. He also continued helping Bresee edit the *Nazarene Messenger*. However, much of his activity was now conducted under the auspices of the NHA and on an interdenominational basis.

C. W. Ruth

As he traveled, Ruth grew burdened by the small and often parochial Holiness bodies he found scattered across the United States. He made the initial contacts that brought the Church of the Nazarene (West) into association with the Association of Pentecostal Churches of America (East). These contacts paved the way for the merger of the two denominations at Chicago in October 1907—the First General Assembly. In the spring of 1908, he held a revival at Texas Holiness University near Greenville, Texas, where he also promoted the consolidation of the Holiness forces into one church. His work there led to Bresee's invitation to visit the school a few weeks later, where the first permanent Nazarene congregation in Texas was organized. Ruth likewise brokered the union of the Pennsylvania Conference of the Holiness Christian Church with the Pentecostal Church of the Nazarene in September 1908, by exerting influence on his

Standing in front of Canaan Hall at Olivet.
C. W. Ruth is in the middle. Bud Robinson is to his right.

old friends and colleagues, Jonas and Horace Trumbaur, leaders of the Pennsylvania group. And he made the initial contacts with C. B. Jernigan of the Holiness Church of Christ (South), which resulted in the presence of Southern delegates to the First General Assembly at Chicago in 1907 and paved the way for the Second General Assembly to be held at Pilot Point, Texas, where the union of churches culminated the following year. All the mergers that took place between October 1907 and October 1908, creating the Pentecostal Church of the Nazarene as a national body, had C. W. Ruth's fingerprints all over them.

Ruth continued his interdenominational ministry through the National Holiness Association, and as the denomination he helped knit together began to develop its own sectarian tendencies, Ruth again showed the way to balance institutional needs with sensitivity and openness to Christians of other denominations. In 1908, he accepted a leadership role in the NHA to become "the right-hand man" of president C. J. Fowler for the rest of the decade. In 1910, he was instrumental in establishing the NHA's missionary arm, the National Holiness Missionary Society, which he later served as president from 1925 until his death in 1941.

He showed his opposition to sectarian holiness in other ways, too. For nearly six months, he served as interim pastor of the Pilgrim Holiness congregation in Pasadena, California, despite the fact that the congregation had resulted several years before in a split within the Southern California District of the Church of the Nazarene. And he served as a long-time trustee of Asbury College in Wilmore, Kentucky, a non-denominational college rooted in the broad Wesleyan-Holiness movement. Ruth died there on the Asbury campus. His body was returned to Pasadena, where he had moved several years before his death, and he was buried with the California Nazarenes he had come to love so dearly many years before.

The scores of tributes published after his death bore eloquent testimony to the fact that this man—so pivotal in the formation of the Church of the Nazarene—was a Nazarene equally-well remembered for his work in interdenominational holiness.

### John Short
***Pastor of the Cambridge Church of the Nazarene***

John Short, A. B. Riggs, and H. N. Brown were dubbed the "Three Wise Men from the East" by the early Nazarenes. They were New England

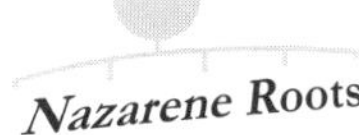


pastors with prominent roles in the Holiness Movement along America's eastern seaboard. They earned their nickname by crossing America in 1906 to explore merger between their own Association of Pentecostal Churches of America and Bresee's Church of the Nazarene on the opposite coast. The visit was fruitful, Bresee journeyed east the next year, and plans were laid for the First General Assembly of a new denomination that united holiness churches on both coasts.

John Short

The "wise men" had significant New England Holiness ministries, and John Short's was in historic Cambridge, MA, where he enjoyed a distinguished 28-year pastorate near Harvard University.

Short was born in rural Massachusetts in 1841 to immigrant parents from Scotland and Ireland. Converted at age 12, he felt called to preach six years later. He tested this call by ministering for two years in the Troy Conference of the Methodist Episcopal Church. Satisfied that the call was genuine, Short entered Boston University School of Theology to prepare more thoroughly for his lifetime of pastoral ministry.

He entered the New England Conference upon graduating, and Bishop Wiley ordained him an elder in 1873. A string of Methodist pastorates followed, including those in Reading, Stoneham, East Cambridge, Lowell, and Beverly. He became active in the Holiness Movement. At Asbury Grove Camp near Hamilton, MA, he professed the grace of entire sanctification under Alfred Cookman's preaching. Short eventually assumed responsibility for Asbury Grove Holiness Camp and took a significant role in the Douglas Camp Meeting, one of the better-known and better-attended eastern Holiness camps, which he served for many years as vice-president. Short's contributions to the Holiness cause are well-documented in the *Christian Witness,* the paper of the National Holiness Association, published in nearby Boston.

John Short

These activities gradually drew Short away from the M. E. Church. In 1894, he transferred to the Evangelical Association, a German Methodist denomination with a stronger commitment to Christian perfection. But Short had grown tired of the Methodist itinerant system, whereby bishops appoint pastors to churches and move them on a regular basis. He made another change in 1900 into the Association of Pentecostal Churches of America, a Holiness denomination with a congregational government. There, he found the congenial company of William Howard Hoople, H. F. Reynolds, Susan Fitkin, and many others.

Short's ministry in Cambridge began in 1894 as a home mission project of the Evangelical Association. His decision to leave the Evangelical

Association led to an unfortunate split in the congregation, for many of its members wanted to follow Short and continue under his pastoral guidance. Short organized them into the Cambridge Pentecostal Church, and they worshiped in a rented hall for several years. In 1914, they erected a new $15,000 building just off Cambridge's central square, where the Cambridge Church of the Nazarene still worships today.

Intensely pietistic but also intellectual, Short led the congregation until his death in 1922. He was regarded as one of the finest preachers in the Nazarene movement. A successor wrote: "No moral break marred his character, no indiscretions brought shame and sorrow to his friends. . . . He was the soul of integrity and sincerity. He never exploited a financial scheme that hurt his influence and his friends. . . . He was the kind of man the world and the church need today."

Hiram F. Reynolds

Dr. and Mrs. Reynolds, 1904

**Hiram F. Reynolds**
***Casting the Vision***

Early Nazarenes faced a central dilemma: How could several Holiness bodies, arising in different regions of the United States, and each a fully independent and self-governing denomination, function as a united body after the mergers that knitted them together in 1907 and 1908?

Among those who understood the fundamental problem were C. W. Ruth, who brokered the church marriages; Phineas F. Bresee, whose charisma was significant in the mergers of spirit and constitutional authority; and the energetic Hiram F. Reynolds, whose role in shaping a common denominational outlook became crucial after the Second General Assembly.

Reynolds was the best-traveled Nazarene of his day, promoting the interests of the whole church and stamping it with a vision for worldwide mission.

Hiram F. Reynolds was born in Lyons, IL, on May 12, 1854. His early years were spent in the area's rural communities around Chicago and on prairies west of the city. Reynolds recalled those years: "Well do I remember as I lay on my straw tick in the garret, how my little heart would beat with fear as the packs of wolves would gather about the humble shack of a house and howl until father or brothers or all would go out and drive them away."

Reynolds' father suffered an early death, and extreme poverty forced the widowed mother to make painful choices. The older children either moved into Chicago to begin making their way in the world, or were placed in good homes where they could earn their keep. The latter became Hiram's fate. Many years later, he admonished Nazarenes to support their children's General Orphanage Board, reminding them that "God has declared himself Father of the fatherless."

Hiram F. Reynolds

Reynolds grew to manhood apart from church or creed, but at 20, he moved to Chicago and boarded with his oldest brother's family. The family were Methodists. The vital Christian faith of Reynolds' brother caught his attention, but his sister-in-law's faith impressed him even more. He later regarded her influence as a providential leading toward his eventual salvation.

In 1874, he went to Vermont to visit his mother and youngest brother. It was only the second time he had seen them in nearly a decade. He remained there for some time. There, he was converted among the Methodists, called to preach, and entered Montpelier Theological Seminary. In 1879, he began his ministry.

Hiram F. and Mrs. Reynolds

Reynolds served various churches in the Vermont Conference: Bondville, Plymouth Notch, Barnard, Topshen Circuit, and the Chelsea-West Chelsea charge. In 1886, he was ordained an elder by Bishop John F. Hurst (who 11 years later ordained J. G. Morrison—Reynolds' successor on the Board of General Superintendents—an elder in the Northern Minnesota Conference). In 1879, Reynolds married Stella Byerd. They had three children: Eliza Belle, Stella Ardelia, and Aaron. Many years later, they adopted a granddaughter, Frances.

Reynolds became active in the work of the Vermont Holiness Association, serving as its president. In 1892, he sought release from pastoral ministry in order to engage fully in revivalism, turning aside an offer to serve his conference as presiding elder (district superintendent). Three years later, so his revival work could have unhindered rein, he withdrew from the Methodist Episcopal Church and became the first episcopally ordained clergyman to unite with the fledgling Association of Pentecostal Churches of America. At the first assembly of the APCA in 1897, he was elected Home and Foreign Missions secretary—a position he retained until the First General Assembly of the Pentecostal Church of the Nazarene in 1907, when Reynolds' group united with Bresee's group in the west.

Reynolds wore two hats for most of his subsequent career: general superintendent (1907-32) and chief executive of the General Board

Reynolds with missionaries and national workers in Japan

of Foreign Missions (1908-22; 1925-27). From this position of dual responsibility, Reynolds strengthened the connectional bonds between the newly united regions of the church. He became an incessant traveler, presiding at district assemblies, preaching in camp meetings, and conducting the business of the church. He carried a portable typewriter and typed his correspondence, pounding away even on the train as he went along. He published reports simultaneously in the church's three regional papers until *Herald of Holiness* was founded in 1912 as a denomination-wide paper. Reynolds moved his family residence with some frequency—Brooklyn, Chicago, Oklahoma City, Kansas City—so that various sections of the church would feel personal contact with the general superintendency.

"In truth no one can be a great preacher without first being a great Christian."

Missions was his trademark cause, advocated at every district assembly that Reynolds conducted. His advocacy helped unify the church by holding out to it a larger vision centered on a biblical theme. In 1913-14,

Hiram F. Reynolds – *Slow Train in China*

he visited the churches and missions in Japan, China, India, and Africa, encouraging and strengthening them. His round-the-world trip was an event followed with interest by the Nazarene public through his reports in *Herald of Holiness* and the monthly missions periodical, *The Other Sheep.* Many of Reynolds' original photographs were later published in a book about the trip.

Subsequent travels took him repeatedly across North America, and to the Middle East, the Caribbean, Central America, and back to Japan and China. His colleague, J. B. Chapman, praised Reynolds as "the original foreign missionary of the Nazarene movement." He added: "We, as a church and people, owe more to the early vision, enthusiasm, and zeal of H. F. Reynolds for the success of our missionary enterprise than to any other."

In 1932, Reynolds became general superintendent emeritus, but continued conducting district assemblies on a regular basis until 1934. In 1938, he died at age 84 and was buried in Townshend, VT. The legacy of Hiram F. Reynolds lives on in the hundreds of Nazarene districts that exist in Asia, Africa, the Caribbean, and Latin America.

### Mary Lee Cagle
### ***Pastor and Evangelist***

Mary Wasson's commitment to Christ was made initially in the saving fires of north Alabama revivalism. At 15, she knelt beside her brother Frank at a Methodist mourner's bench. The experience of divine grace, so deep and powerful, created an evangelist's heart; and over the next year, Mary worked to bring her classmates to faith in Christ.

H. C. Cagle, Mary Lee Cagle, Fannie McDowell Hunter, Trena Platt

Her call to ministry grew more certain over time. To the consternation of family and friends, Mary testified to a call to preach, but the Methodist Church of the 1880s did not ordain women to the ministry nor allow them to preach. Preaching was "man's work." And in the hierarchical South, women were not to "step out of their place." Mary's mother was mortified by her testimony. An older brother threatened to keep his children from her. She finally bowed to social pressure, muted her testimony, and conformed to the expectations of church and society. She became a schoolteacher.

She carried a heavy burden for this conformity. An uneasy conscience stood between her and God. It plagued her spiritual life. She later looked back on this period with deep regret and condemned her own "man-fearing spirit." No altar work with others, no other bargain with God assuaged her guilt.

"We make a high profession, and may the Lord help us to live up to what we profess—is my prayer."

Mary was in her late 20s when a liberating path opened up. Robert Lee Harris, a Holiness revivalist, held meetings near Landersville, Alabama. She heard his message, sought the experience of holiness, and found a deeper experience of grace. The next year, when Harris returned to the area, they married.

She had never stepped outside Lawrence County, Alabama. Now she became her husband's constant companion and accompanied him everywhere. Contact with Nashville, Memphis, and other southern cities added new dimensions to her worldly understanding.

She learned Robert Lee Harris' message and methods, absorbing the idioms and accent of Holiness revivalism. They collaborated on songs. And in an area east of Memphis, they planted Calvary holiness bands—circles of disciples who embraced the religion of the heart that R. L. Harris preached so earnestly.

But there was still that problem about the old "man-fearing spirit." In 1894, R. L. Harris left the Methodist Episcopal Church, South, to organize a Holiness church with a congregational form of government in Milan, Tennessee. He suffered from tuberculosis, however, and died in November.

Mary Lee Cagle and Trena Platt

Mary Lee Harris faced a crucial decision. Her mother pled with her to return to Alabama, but she embraced a different decision. She answered the call to preach that came more intensely than ever. Her early sermons were delivered timidly. Months passed before she felt liberty in preaching.

Other events followed. She and Donie Mitchum organized several congregations and the connection of churches began growing. The work expanded into Arkansas and north Alabama, and by 1896, Mary had planted congregations in west Texas. Miss Trena Platt traveled with Mary Harris as her musician for several years.

The number of ministers increased, first women—Elliott J. Sheeks, Fannie McDowell Hunter, and Annie May Johnson—and then men—George Hammond, William E. Fisher, and J. A. Murphree. A structure evolved. The first general meeting was held in Milan in 1899, and the business

items included the ordinations of Mary Harris, Elliott Sheeks, and George Hammond.

Mary Lee Harris' work in Texas consumed more of her time. A Baptist preacher described her ministry in Abilene, where she preached to an estimated 800 to 1,000 people at a time: "Mrs. Harris knows how to preach. There is an absence of the usual excitement prevailing at most of the tent or camp meetings, but for deep feeling and willingness to respond to the invitation extended, it equals the best protracted meetings I ever attended in Abilene." And to those with doubts about the "scripturalness of woman preaching," he added: "It would be infinitely better to have our boys and girls irregularly saved, than to fall regularly into a Christless grave."

In 1900, she moved her home to Buffalo Gap, near Abilene. She had other interests there too. That summer, she married Henry Cagle in front of hundreds gathered at the Buffalo Gap camp meeting. He was a rough-and-tumble cowboy who had been converted, sanctified, and called to preach through her ministry.

H.C. and Mary Lee Cagle

In 1902, Mary Lee Cagle convened the first annual meeting of the Texas Council of the New Testament Church of Christ. Twelve churches were represented. From that point, the Texas Council was differentiated from the Eastern Council, composed of churches in Tennessee and Arkansas. Cagle travelled between the two councils to maintain some focus of unity. An associate took her measure in 1904, writing: "She is here and there and everywhere in the interest of missions and the church generally." Nearly a third of the New Testament Church of Christ's ministers were women, often called to preach under Mary Cagle's ministry.

In 1904, the New Testament churches merged with a group led by C. B. Jernigan. The new body, the Holiness Church of Christ, merged four years later with the Pentecostal Church of the Nazarene. Mary Cagle was involved in both mergers. The Texas Council became the Abilene (now West Texas) District of the Church of the Nazarene. Charles McConnell, editor of a Holiness paper, dubbed her "the mother of holiness in West Texas."

Mary and Henry Cagle kept pushing the frontiers of Holiness revivalism. They planted a strong church in Lubbock, Texas, organized

H.C. and Mary Lee Cagle

churches in New Mexico, and conducted revivals and organized churches as far north as Wyoming. She served as District Evangelist on the New Mexico and Abilene Districts. Her report to the district assembly in 1927 underscored her concerns: "Our work has not been with the larger churches, but with the weak struggling ones. I have held 13 revival meetings, preached 175 times, saw 216 converted and 118 sanctified. . . . I have [visited] practically all of the churches in the district and some of them more than once."

She was a delegate to each General Assembly through 1928, the year her autobiography was published.

She preached for the last time at 90. Then blind and weak, two strong men helped her stand as she delivered a 30-minute sermon with "her usual vim and enthusiasm." The "man-fearing spirit" was long dead. The religion of the heart was everything. She died the next year.

### George Sharpe
### *The Pentecostal Church of Scotland*

George Sharpe

Early Methodism spread under John Wesley's inspired leadership from England into neighboring Wales, Scotland, and Ireland, and then to the Americas. The American Holiness Movement reversed the direction a century later, sending Phoebe Palmer, Charles G. Finney, Hannah Whitall Smith and other trans-Atlantic revivalists to Great Britain.

The Atlantic connection proved equally fateful to Nazarene origins in the British Isles, and George Sharpe was the pivotal figure in this equation.

Sharpe was born April 17, 1865, near Craigneuk, Lanarkshire, Scotland. A miner's son, he entered the work force at age 12. By 14, he was a clerk in the office of a steelworks company.

Sharpe experienced an evangelical conversion in 1882 and, by age 20, sensed a call to preach. He did not act on the conviction; instead he accepted an American industrialist's invitation to be trained as an industrial manager at the latter's company in Cortland, NY. Sharpe arrived there in early 1886, only to discover that the American firm had scrapped its plan to build a factory in France while Sharpe was at sea. His grand opportunity vanished with that decision!

He began attending a Methodist Church. The call to preach returned with greater urgency. Local Methodists affirmed his gifts and encouraged

him to take the step. He finally submitted to the call, took ministerial training, entered the Northern New York Conference of the Methodist Episcopal Church, and was ordained an elder by Bishop FitzGerald in 1893.

Over the next 14 years, he pastored Methodist churches in Depeyster, Hamilton, and Chateaugay, NY. He was sanctified during the Chateaugay pastorate in a revival conducted by L. Milton Williams. Sharpe was aligned unswervingly with the Holiness Movement thereafter.

He took his family to Scotland for a vacation in 1901. While there, he was invited to be pastor of the Congregational church in Ardrossan. Viewing this as an opportunity to preach the Holiness message in his native land, he accepted the call, laboring at Ardrossan until 1905, when he was called to be minister to the Parkhead Congregational Church in Glasgow.

Parkhead Congregational prospered under Sharpe's leadership, but tensions developed with some leading members. At issue were Sharpe's Methodist style and unequivocal message of Christian holiness. He was evicted as pastor in 1906, but some 80 members rallied to his side.

In October, the Parkhead Pentecostal Church was organized under his leadership. Similar congregations were formed in the ensuing months in Paisley, Uddington, and other places. In 1909, the growing network of Holiness congregations formed the Pentecostal Church of Scotland. Its *Manual* was influenced partly by the 1908 *Manual* of the Pentecostal Church of the Nazarene. Sharpe served as the Pentecostal Church of Scotland's general leader until 1915.

The new denomination faced many decisions. How should it respond, for instance, to the application of Olive Winchester, an American theology student at the University of Glasgow, who sought ordination? Sharpe supported the decision in 1912 to ordain her. Winchester became the first woman ordained to the ministry in Scotland by any church group and went on to a distinguished career at Northwest Nazarene College and Pasadena College. (Jane Sharpe, George's wife, often preached in his absence and was ordained in 1917).

In 1915, Sharpe guided the Pentecostal Church of Scotland to union with the Pentecostal Church of the Nazarene. The union gave the latter its first foothold in Europe, while the Pentecostal Church of Scotland gained the advantage of an international fellowship. The churches in Scotland were reorganized as the British Isles District, which Sharpe led as superintendent from 1915-24 and 1928-32.

He also served from 1923-26 as regional missionary superintendent overseeing Nazarene churches and mission work in Africa, India, and the Middle East. In this capacity, he strongly encouraged the plan to build Raleigh Fitkin Memorial Hospital at Manzini, Swaziland—a project to which his daughter and son-in-law, medical missionaries Kanema and David Hynd, devoted their lives to building and sustaining. George and Jane Sharpe participated in the hospital's groundbreaking ceremony.

He returned to the pastorate when his second tenure as British Isles district superintendent ended, serving Parkhead Church of the Nazarene again (1932-38) and enjoying interim pastorates at the Motherwell Church of the Nazarene. His death on March 27, 1948, a few months after the death of General Superintendent Chapman, was another indication that the era of the Church of the Nazarene's founders had come to a close.

# Chapter 4

# *Shaping the Nazarene Way*

## Introduction

The people profiled in this chapter played a primary role in shaping the character of ideas and institutions within the Church of the Nazarene in its first century. Some were founders, while others had their ministry in the church's second and third generations. Each contributed to the emerging mosaic of Nazarene culture.

These pastors, missionaries, evangelists, educators and laity are representative of hundreds of others who labored to build Nazarene churches, missions, and colleges. But they are also distinguished by the excellence with which they pursued their ministries and discipleship.

As the preacher on "La Hora Nazarena" radio broadcast, H. T. Reza developed a ministry that projected Nazarene influence and the Wesleyan-Holiness message from over 600 radio stations in Central, South, and North America. Susan Fitkin developed skills as an evangelist that she applied to building the Church of the Nazarene's general missionary society. Robert Pierce entered pastoral ministry at midlife as a second career; but when he came into contact with Bresee and the Nazarenes in Los Angeles, he used skills acquired in his first trade—the publishing industry—to help Bresee keep *The Nazarene Messenger* on its weekly schedule. C. J. Kinne was another experienced pastor who went on to launch the Nazarene Publishing House of Kansas City and build a Nazarene hospital in China. After a long pastoral career in the Methodist Episcopal Church, South, B. F. Haynes used his editorial and theological skills as founding editor of *Herald of Holiness*, the Church of the Nazarene's flagship periodical. C. A. McConnell was a committed layman whose devotion to publishing and missions resulted in the founding of *The Other Sheep* magazine, which he edited. It kept early Nazarenes fully informed about the missions, missionaries, and national workers around the world, whom their tithes supported, convincing early generations of the church that sacrificial giving to the church's general ministries was money well-spent. H. Orton Wiley began exerting a theological influence on the Church of the Nazarene in the mid-1920s when J. B. Chapman gave him a platform through the pages of *The Preacher's Magazine.* Wiley used the opportunity to keep pastors up-to-date on various branches of theology—especially biblical, historical, and systematic theology. Wiley's influence extended even farther after the publication of his three-volume *Christian Theology* in the early 1940s. It remained a basic theological text in clergy preparation for the next half-century. Timothy Smith pastored a congregation in New England while simultaneously teaching American religious history at a leading American university in Maryland. He brought Harvard training and his own keen insight to his analysis of Nazarene origins and early development.

"The Nazarene way" emphasized evangelism, cross-cultural missions, literature, compassionate ministry, and education as the critical methods by which the church was to carry out the denominational mission. Each strand was related directly to the church's focus on holiness of heart and life. Like John Wesley, the Nazarenes turned to those who were "like sheep without a shepherd" and offered them Christ. They built colleges to educate pastors and laity, and they started theological seminaries so that they could, in Chapman's words, reach out with "more preachers and better preachers." In solidarity with Christ, they met the needs of the poor through orphanages, maternity homes, hospitals, clinics, and inner-city rescue missions. They believed in literature. Every Nazarene family in 1935 that subscribed to *Herald of Holiness* and *The Other Sheep* received over 170 pages of Nazarene periodical reading each month. Nazarenes worked together, pooling financial resources through the church's connectional system, enabling local churches to multiply their impact by supporting general, district, and regional ministries.

## M. D. Wood and India
### *The Dawn of Nazarene Missions*

Five missionaries sailed from New York City on December 11, 1897. In London, they visited John Wesley's old City Road chapel before boarding the steamer "Egypt," which took them across the Mediterranean, through the Gulf of Suez, around Aden, and on to India. They disembarked in Bombay on January 14 and, within days, established a mission in Igatpuri, 85 miles northeast. The Nazarene mission era had begun!

Rev. Martyn D. Wood

Rev. Martyn D. Wood was the mission superintendent. He and Anna, his wife, had served in India earlier under another missionary board. Lillian Sprague, Carrie Taylor, and Fred Wiley—all New Englanders—rounded out the group.

Their sponsor was the Association of Pentecostal Churches of America, an eastern Holiness denomination. Its oldest congregation was not even 11 years old. Indeed, its New England churches had merged with those in New York only the previous year. And yet, the young denomination was already missionary-minded!

Its "home missions" thrust soon carried the APCA into Canada and as far west as Iowa. Its world mission program—coordinated by Hiram F. Reynolds—would soon result in missions in Cape Verde and other places. The Igatpuri mission, then, was the first fruit of an evangelistic vision unbounded by region, nation, age, or race.

Anna Wood

Wood and the missionary band immediately encountered India's many orphaned children. In February, they accepted 16 orphans—all that they felt they could reasonably support. A severe famine in 1899 would multiply the numbers of India's orphans. Their need—always confronting the missionaries—was consistently mentioned in their weekly letters to America.

What was mission life like? Anna Wood took charge of the dispensary, administering "simple remedies." Lillian Sprague headed the school, where the orphans were taught with other children. M. D. Wood and Fred Wiley developed preaching points. Wood reported that on April 2—less than 3 months after settling in Igatpuri—he baptized ten men and boys, nine of them converts through their ministry.

It was not all unbounded success. The missionaries were often sick. Wiley and Miss Taylor married, and in the summer of 1899 severed their connection to the APCA, leaving to take charge of a mission in Raj Nandgam run by another religious group. Mina Shroyer, who joined the

Leighton S. Tracy

group in late 1898, also left after a brief term of service.

In September 1899, the Woods, Lillian Sprague, and the orphaned children left Igatpuri and relocated in Buldana, Berar. They re-established their routines on property loaned by the Church Missionary Society (the missionary arm of the Church of England). By this time, Wood was holding four religious services a week in Marathi and one in English. The routine continued until the missionaries furloughed in 1903.

They returned in 1904 with nine others, including Leighton S. Tracy and Gertrude Perry. The new force included the redoubtable Julia Gibson, later an ordained minister *and* physician.

A new location was purchased outside Buldana, while Perry and her mother, Ella, started a mission in Chikli, to the south. In 1905, Tracy and Perry were married.

L. S. Tracy Family

And then disaster! Three of the new missionaries returned to America within the year, while M. D. Wood grew increasingly unhappy in his relationship to the APCA's missionary board. In February 1905, the Woods, two other missionaries, the orphans, and all the national workers, took the livestock and walked away from Buldana and out of Nazarene history to start an independent work that did not prosper.

Five missionaries were left. At Buldana: the Tracys and Gertrude's mother, Ella. At Chikli: Julia Gibson and Priscilla Hitchens. Wood had left the deeds to the two mission properties and a note of farewell.

Patiently, the five missionaries began rebuilding the work. In 1907, Miss Hitchens reopened work in Igatpuri after property there was deeded

Nazarene Young Peoples Society, India, 1933

to the APCA. That same year, the creation at Chicago of the Pentecostal Church of the Nazarene through the APCA's merger with the Church of the Nazarene brought them into relation to the latter's mission in Calcutta, an indigenous work which Bresee's church had adopted in 1906.

And even more prospects! In 1908, the Pentecostal Nazarene merger with the Holiness Church of Christ infused new workers into the field, including Rev. and Mrs. L. A. Campbell, who joined the Buldana mission.

Musicians

There is a natural denouement to this story. Tracy had met the requirements to be an ordained minister, but had never actually been ordained. The need to do this prompted the first general gathering of workers from the three parent bodies of the united church. On June 27, 1909, L. A. Campbell, authorized to act in place of the general superintendents, laid hands on Tracy's head and ordained him as an elder in the Pentecostal Church of the Nazarene.

The Igatpuri-Buldana mission was the opening. The Woods and those with them laid the first foundations and secured the properties in Buldana and Chikli that would prove strategic for future development. Just as importantly, their work signaled the clear intention of those who had sent them to be part of an international fellowship of Christian believers.

Bible School Students Studying in Basim, India

**Susan Fitkin**
***Mother of Nazarene Missions***

The Woman's Missionary Society was authorized by the General Assembly of 1915 as the missionary auxiliary of the Pentecostal Church of the Nazarene. The organization quickly joined the deaconess movement

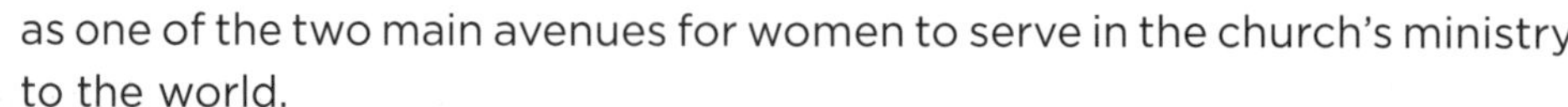

as one of the two main avenues for women to serve in the church's ministry to the world.

Susan Fitkin

Much of the inspiration and leadership of the early WMS sprang from the Rev. Susan Norris Fitkin. Her ability to articulate a missionary vision and to inspire others was rooted in her personal experience as an evangelist and pastor.

Susan Norris was a Canadian, born March 31, 1870, on a farm near Ely, Quebec. Her Quaker parents were active in the temperance reform movement. Her mother served once as a delegate to the Women's Christian Temperance Union convention in Ottawa.

In 1881, the family moved to East Farnham, Quebec, where Susan's parents held longstanding membership in a Quaker meeting house. She, too, attended Quaker worship, but also visited an Anglican church. Later, she began attending the Union Chapel, an interdenominational church that was strongly evangelical in emphasis. Each different strain of piety nourished her spiritual development. Several encounters with life-threatening illnesses, including typhoid fever, heightened her seriousness toward religion. At times, she experienced unusual dreams and saw visions.

Susan Fitkin, Mrs. Willis Fitkin, A. E. Fitkin Jr.

In 1890, she offered herself as a missionary to the China Inland Mission, but was refused for health reasons. She began conducting services for youth in her community and then, at her mother's urging, in other communities. Out of this, her career as an evangelist began to emerge in 1892. She attended a Christian Endeavor meeting in New York City, where she met J. Walter Malone, leader in a fast-growing Holiness wing of the Society of Friends.

Susan Fitkin with Emma Wood

Norris subsequently attended Malone's school, Friends' Bible Institute and Training School in Cleveland. While there, she began preaching in revivals. In 1893, she became pastor of a church in Vermont, where she had previously conducted a revival. Another pastorate followed in the Green Mountains. By that point, she was listed as a "recorded" (or official) minister in the Friends Church. In 1895, at the urging of a leading New York Quaker, Susan Fitkin returned to evangelism. That fall, she was sanctified in a revival and paired for six months with Abram E. Fitkin. Was someone playing matchmaker? The sources do not say, but Susan Norris and A. E. Fitkin were married by a Quaker minister on May 14, 1896.

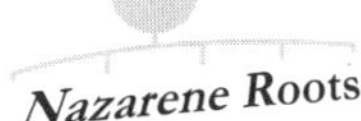


By that date, the two evangelists filed regular reports of their work in *The Christian Witness,* a leading Holiness journal and organ of the National Holiness Association. In late 1896, they organized an independent congregation of 60 members in Hopewell Junction, NY, at the conclusion of a revival. Since the new church was mostly non-Quaker in background, the Fitkins steered it toward affiliation with the Association of Pentecostal Churches of America, the Nazarene parent-body in the East, which they, too, joined.

Susan Fitkin with Emma Wood

Until A. E. Fitkin embarked on a new career on Wall Street in 1903, he and Susan served the APCA as evangelists. In 1899 and 1900, Susan Fitkin helped write a constitution for the APCA's existing women's missionary auxiliary. She was then elected its president. Between 1900 and 1907, that group grew from about 75 members to nearly 400.

The church unions of 1907 and 1908 devolved the Eastern group's missionary auxiliaries to the status of mere local societies. That status was not acceptable to many women, Susan Fitkin chief among them, who began raising denominational consciousness of the need for an organized mission auxiliary. It took seven years, but their vision was realized in 1915, when the Fourth General Assembly authorized them to draw up a constitution for a general society. The constitution was approved in 1919.

Abram and Susan Fitkin

Susan Fitkin was elected as the organization's first president. She served in that office until 1948, utilizing her skills as preacher and evangelist in the advocacy of missions. Under her direction, WMS chapters were formed across North America and Great Britain, and soon across the whole world—Japan, China, India, Syria. The society in Tamingfu, China, for instance, was organized as early as 1922. The international character of the society made it a vehicle through which women from diverse cultures and nationalities discovered and expressed a sense of solidarity in pursuit of common interests and purposes. Fitkin traveled extensively on behalf of the work, visiting Japan, China, India, Africa, Mexico, Great Britain, and other places.

Susan Fitkin

The society's name changed over the years: Woman's Foreign Missionary Society, Nazarene World Missionary Society, and Nazarene Missions International—among others. With the admission of men into membership in the 1970s, its character changed as well.

Susan Norris Fitkin died in California in 1951, leaving a lasting legacy to the Church of the Nazarene.

## Robert Pierce
***Bresee's Englishman***

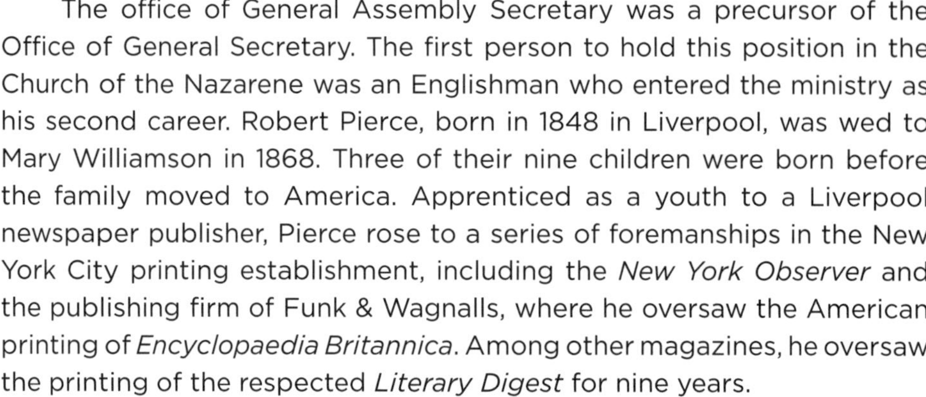

The office of General Assembly Secretary was a precursor of the Office of General Secretary. The first person to hold this position in the Church of the Nazarene was an Englishman who entered the ministry as his second career. Robert Pierce, born in 1848 in Liverpool, was wed to Mary Williamson in 1868. Three of their nine children were born before the family moved to America. Apprenticed as a youth to a Liverpool newspaper publisher, Pierce rose to a series of foremanships in the New York City printing establishment, including the *New York Observer* and the publishing firm of Funk & Wagnalls, where he oversaw the American printing of *Encyclopaedia Britannica*. Among other magazines, he oversaw the printing of the respected *Literary Digest* for nine years.

Robert Pierce

Pierce was a deeply religious man who abandoned his successful career in the publishing trade to enter the ministry. He took this step in the 1880s and served a series of pastorates in the New York East Conference of the Methodist Episcopal Church. One of his parishes included the Woodstock M.E. Church in New York City. His social conscience was awakened, and Pierce labored in urban rescue missions, including a Florence Crittenden mission for unwed mothers and evangelist Jerry McAuley's famous mission on Water Street, which helped the homeless and addicts. Around 1890, Pierce took charge of Hadley Rescue Mission in Salem, MA, and led it for nearly five years.

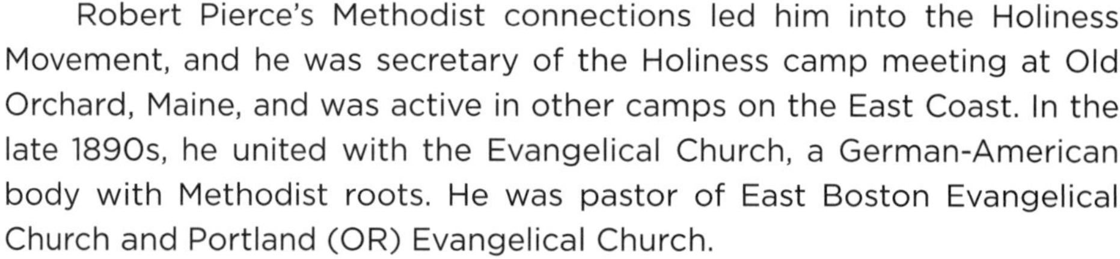

Robert Pierce's Methodist connections led him into the Holiness Movement, and he was secretary of the Holiness camp meeting at Old Orchard, Maine, and was active in other camps on the East Coast. In the late 1890s, he united with the Evangelical Church, a German-American body with Methodist roots. He was pastor of East Boston Evangelical Church and Portland (OR) Evangelical Church.

At the close of his Portland pastorate in 1903, Pierce united with the Church of the Nazarene and was founding pastor of Boise First Church before serving in Oakland, CA. He moved to Los Angeles and was pastor of several area churches while working simultaneously for five years as office editor of the *Nazarene Messenger*, a forerunner of *Herald of Holiness*. While Bresee was listed as the paper's editor, it was Pierce who oversaw the actual production of each weekly issue, and he wrote some of its editorial content.

At the General Assemblies of 1907 and 1908, Robert Pierce was elected

General Assembly Secretary. He edited the official printed proceedings of both events and worked on the *Manual* revisions that were ordered. He was the author of numerous booklets and tracts, including *Apples of Gold*, a popular collection of spiritual gems originally published in the *Nazarene Messenger*. Pierce also taught homiletics at Pasadena College in its early years. He died in Los Angeles in 1937.

Robert Pierce

His deep concern for social work was evident in this passage written for *Herald of Holiness* in 1913.

> We are aware that very few individual churches can support a rescue mission; but where there are three or four of our churches in one city or its surroundings, there ought to be no difficulty as to its support—either in reference to its financial needs, or to the supply of godly men and women to carry on its work; then, if that is not possible, there ought to be one or two at least in each assembly district located in the most populous cities. . . . Our families are tenderly cared for by the church, and that is right; but I make a plea for the other end of the line—the sinking and submerged tenth. I believe this great and trying work belongs to the church, which it has so long neglected. . . . What church is better able to undertake this work than the Pentecostal Church of the Nazarene, with its deep spiritual life and bright joyous methods. . . . Let there be a deeper bond of sympathy between the church and rescue mission, and the financial question will take care of itself. (*Herald of Holiness*, March 19, 1930).

**C. J. Kinne**
***Publisher and Missionary***

In his study of the populist movement of late 19th-century America, social historian Lawrence Goodwyn identified critical factors in the success or failure of any movement seeking to organize itself and propagate a distinctive ideology that contrasts with established patterns of thought. One is the necessity of internal lines of communication that facilitate the mass educational processes and carry news of internal developments in the movement's struggle to define its purpose and mission. In the Wesleyan-Holiness agitation of the same period, Holiness journalism played this role

of promoting cohesion and solidarity, and continued to do so during the turn-of-the-century transition from "a Holiness Movement" to "Holiness churches."

C. J. and Susan Kinne

C. J. Kinne instinctively understood the role of the press in developing a sense of "movement identity" during the movement years, and a sense of connectional identity during the denominational years.

Born in Iowa in 1869, Kinne became a Methodist preacher around 1890. Five years later, he united with Bresee's Nazarene movement on the West Coast, soon becoming business manager of the Nazarene Messenger Company, and accepting a salary less than half his previous one. In this capacity, he worked closely with Bresee in the editorial work and oversaw the production of a weekly paper, books, and—after 1907—Sunday school curriculum.

In 1911, three years after the merger of regional churches into the Pentecostal Church of the Nazarene, Kinne played a leading role in bringing together his company with the Pentecostal Advocate Company of Greenville, TX. This process led to the formation of the Pentecostal Nazarene Publishing House. A member of the General Assembly committee that made these recommendations, Kinne was involved in selecting Kansas City as the site for the new venture and was elected as its first manager. He moved to Kansas City, organized the company, purchased its equipment, and began publishing the church's paper and literature under the restraints of limited finances.

Nazarene Publishing Company in Los Angeles, 1912. Kinne is seated in the middle. Robert Pierce is to his left.

C. A. McConnell worked closely with him during these years and later wrote that Kinne was "the Columbus of our publishing interests." McConnell continued:

> He knew that if the recently merged streams of Holiness thought and experience from the West, the East, and the South should ever become a denomination, one in ideas as well as in ideals, it would be such through the literature of a common publishing house. Kinne's idea became a purpose, and the purpose a fact. . . . To those of us who were his coworkers in the beginning, how near it appeared to be the 'making of bricks without straw'—or clay.
>
> That was the spring of the deep snow. How cold it was in that old residence building, with its two floors, attic, and basement. Down in that dark basement were finally installed a cylinder press, a job press, a second-hand linotype machine, two imposing stones, and a small cabinet of type.
>
> Kinne was General Manager—that is, all the planning, all the hard jobs, all the disagreeable ones, he seemed to consider his own particular property. What a man Kinne was! And how we loved him. It is not a figure of speech to say that he put his life into the foundation of the Publishing House.

C. J. Kinne

Kinne poured himself into the work until he became mentally and emotionally exhausted. Against the wishes of the general superintendents and colleagues, he resigned in 1915 and returned to California. As Kinne recuperated, another idea began to take hold. In time, it would make him the founder of yet a second Nazarene institution.

Kinne became a promoter of the church's cross-cultural missions program, traveling along the West Coast and speaking in Nazarene churches at every opportunity. As he did so, he read widely in mission literature. He became increasingly interested in medical missions. At some point, he began articulating their basis. He noted: "In these times, when real poverty is so rare among [Western] Christians and when persons in the most ordinary circumstances have so many luxuries, the great mass of professing Christians do not realize the necessity for nor the blessedness of self-denial. If we could but get a real glimpse of the world with its suffering and sorrows, we would understand something of our opportunities and obligations. We are sent not only to preach the gospel but to heal the sick . . . [to follow] Jesus in the work of healing."

In 1919, Kinne founded the Nazarene Medical Missionary Union. Its purpose was to promote medical missions generally and to establish hospitals "under the direction of the General Missionary Board" of the Church of the Nazarene.

Kinne's particular passion was to establish a hospital in China. He made his first trip there in 1923, meeting with Nazarene missionaries in Tamingfu, and agreeing to locate the hospital there with the other Nazarene work. He returned to America to raise more funds, then returned to China from 1924 to 1926, where he became construction manager of the project. By 1925, enough portions had been constructed that Bresee Memorial Hospital began receiving its first patients.

Kinne ran out of money before the project was completed. His wife, left behind in America, died during his absence. Kinne returned to the United States and began raising more funds. He married Susan Bresee, the middle-aged and unmarried daughter of Phineas and Maria Bresee. He returned to China in 1928, taking Sue with him, and for the next 18 months labored to complete the project. The hospital was completed in 1930.

In the years that followed, Bresee Memorial Hospital cared not only for the diseased and afflicted, but also trained nurses and provided training opportunities for Chinese physicians. Indeed, it became the hub of a more extended medical enterprise that included "field medicine" supplied by traveling nurses and doctors.

Kinne's first legacy to the church, then, was the Nazarene Publishing House, today a major publisher of Wesleyan-Holiness literature. His second legacy was a Nazarene hospital in China that functioned until the middle of World War II, and the insight that "those who relieve the sufferings of the body always have the most ready access to the hearts" of others.

C. J. Kinne died in 1932 and is buried in Los Angeles in the Bresee family plot, beside Sue.

Charles. A. McConnell

## C. A. McConnell
### *Journalism and the Realities of Faith*

"According to the plan of the temperance people, I received the nomination as representative from my district to the first Legislature of the state of South Dakota. Of course, I expected the hearty opposition of the liquor forces, and I was not disappointed. I had not been mild in my

denunciation of the iniquitous '3% loan sharks.' And they, and even the bankers, joined up with the saloon keepers against me." So too did the "Farmers Union, a cooperative organization," whose national president, "H.L. Loucks, determined to make it into a political party, starting in Dakota where the Union was strong. . . . Then the impossible happened to turn the tide. . . . Archbishop [John] Ireland, of St. Paul, was an ardent prohibitionist. How he ever heard about me, I do not know; but I do know that the Catholics of my district received the word, 'Vote for McConnell.'"

Charles. A. McConnell, 1952

Elected to South Dakota's first legislature, Charles A. McConnell helped write the state's prohibition law and measures affecting education and family homesteads. McConnell was an experienced newsman who was trained in the newspaper writing and publishing business by his father, who owned and published a string of papers in the upper Midwest. At the time South Dakota became a state, McConnell was a self-described "free thinker" who was uncommitted to either church or creed. He, was, though, committed to morality, honest government, and the abolition of the liquor trade.

General Board of Foreign Missions, 1914.
McConnell is standing left of center.

McConnell placed a high value on family ties, so when his father moved to north Texas for health reasons, McConnell abandoned his political career and moved his wife and children south to keep his extended family intact. He began publishing the *Sunset Signal*, the community newspaper of Sunset, TX, where he continued his attacks on the saloon.

He was converted in 1895 through his wife's influence. He testified to the grace of entire sanctification two years later. These became luminous moments through which he lived the remainder of his life.

At the urging of the Holiness Movement's leaders in Texas, this Yankee transplant sold his newspaper and moved to Peniel, a Holiness colony near the city of Greenville. McConnell then used his skills to pursue Holiness journalism, first as an assistant editor and later as senior editor of the *Pentecostal Advocate*, the leading Holiness publication in the Southwest. McConnell was a charter member of the Nazarene congregation that P. F. Bresee organized personally at Peniel in spring 1908, a half-year before the merger assembly at Pilot Point. *The Pentecostal Advocate* became an official organ of the Church of the Nazarene in 1910, after the Nazarene

paper, published at Pilot Point, ceased publication in the interests of promoting harmony and solidarity among the states' Holiness forces.

McConnell now edited one of three official papers of the Church of the Nazarene. From this position, he helped plan its merger with the *Nazarene Messenger* of Los Angeles to create the *Herald of Holiness*. After the Third General Assembly (1911) acted to consolidate the three publishing houses and papers, McConnell moved to Kansas City, where he served as office editor of the *Herald* (1912-16), managing editor of the Publishing House (1916-18), and founding editor of *The Other Sheep* (later *World Mission* magazine) from 1914-18.

The last phase of McConnell's career took a very different turn. Though a layman, he was theologically astute, and from 1920 to 1939 taught on the religion faculty of Bethany-Peniel College (now Southern Nazarene University). He was dean of the religion department for part of that time.

McConnell's life illustrates varied truths. His early career shows that, contrary to a persistent stereotype, the "secular humanist" may in fact stand for public righteousness and morality. His later devotion to Holiness journalism shows that talents shaped by secular tasks can be consecrated through grace to the deepest spiritual purposes. And the fundamental unity of his early and later life was a desire to know and follow the truth, wherever it led.

B. F. Haynes

## B. F. Haynes
## *Launching* Herald of Holiness

The editor of *Methodist Review*, southern Methodism's respected literary and theological journal, wrote in 1890: "It is with pleasure that we review the financial history of the McKendree Church for the year 1889, under the pastoral charge of Rev. B.F. Haynes. The possibilities that lie dormant in many of our Churches should be developed into facts when the example of this Nashville Church is produced . . . . Various sums united make $6,431.94 for the cause of Missions at home and abroad . . . . We find that only one Methodist Church in the United States raised a larger sum than McKendree has raised this year for Missions." He noted that under Haynes' leadership, the congregation's per capita giving of $30.22 for 1,168 members "is an exhibit that is, we believe, without precedent in the history of Methodism in America."

Four years later, the *Memphis Daily Commercial* profiled the notable delegates at the 1894 General Conference of the Methodist Episcopal Church, South. It reported: "Rev. Benjamin Franklin Haynes has been remarkably acceptable as a preacher in the Tennessee conference, very successful in all church work during the nineteen years of his ministry. He has served all grades of appointments, from mountain circuits to McKendree Church, Nashville. From its first number, he has been editor of the *Tennessee Methodist*—put in that responsible position, not at his solicitation but by the will of his brethren. The vote he received for delegate [to this General Conference], 125, is the largest perhaps ever cast in the Tennessee conference. He represents it, and as its representative, he is heard not seldom in the general conference."

B. F. Haynes during the years he edited the *Tennessee Methodist*

By the mid-1890s, B.F. Haynes was an established and aggressive leader in Tennessee Methodism. After a one-year term as presiding elder (district superintendent) of the East Tennessee District, he founded the *Tennessee Methodist* in 1891. It functioned as an official conference publication until 1896, when it became an independent paper under the title of *Zion's Outlook*. In 1900, it was sold to Rev. J.O. McClurkan and the Pentecostal Mission of Nashville.

Some years later, Haynes looked back on his life in the 1890s and wrote: "Editorial work was the delight of my life and the joy of my heart; I really loved the work, and no work in which I ever engaged was so nearly to my taste and inclination. My love for journalism is not only professional, but the very issues which I felt the paper was divinely called to represent were such as appealed to the noblest instincts of my nature." It was a decisive decade for him, and it prepared him to become the founding editor of *Herald of Holiness*.

Benjamin F. Haynes joined the Church of the Nazarene in 1911, ending 35 years in the Methodist ministry. Almost immediately, he was invited to become the founding editor of *Herald of Holiness*, which the Third General Assembly authorized in a move to consolidate three official papers into one.

The primary issues that led Haynes to sever his relationship to Southern Methodism—the doctrine of entire sanctification, his staunch premillennialism, and his ardent advocacy of the prohibition of liquor—all found a new and unhindered outlet in the pages of the *Herald*.

Nevertheless, Haynes never allowed his doctrinal enthusiasms to dominate the *Herald's* agenda. Under his direction, the church paper was broad in scope and provided a forum for diverse—even competing—

B. F. Haynes

voices to be heard within the church. One of the *Herald's* early features was "The Open Parliament," a column that regularly ran for several pages and allowed readers to comment on everything from theology and discipleship, to issues of war and peace, and the Ku Klux Klan.

While diverse perspectives prevailed, the early *Herald's* focus of unity was equally clear in Haynes' view: the Church of the Nazarene existed to proclaim the doctrine of Christian perfection and the *Herald of Holiness* was to be one of its chief vehicles.

Haynes stated the point in the *Herald's* maiden issue: "Only to a paper devoted to the spread of scriptural holiness would [this editor] for a moment consent to devote his time. To this precious cause for nearly twenty years he has been uncompromisingly committed; for its [behalf] he has surrendered all which most men esteem of value in this life; and in it he sees the solitary hope for the maintenance of our civilization, the preservation of the church and the welfare of universal man in this and in the world to come."

## E. F. Walker
### *The Fourth General Superintendent*

E. F. Walker

Methodist preacher John L. Brasher, who knew evangelists by the hundreds, said Edward F. Walker was "the greatest theologian of all evangelists I have known." J. B. Chapman called him "the Peerless Preacher." Paul Rees described him as a "remarkable preacher" of well-prepared sermons, with twinkling eyes and the "look of a cherub" when he preached.

When E. F. Walker united with the Pentecostal Church of the Nazarene in 1908, he had a national reputation as a biblical exegete and Holiness expositor. His election in 1911 as the fourth general superintendent in the denomination's history reflected the wide esteem in which he was held.

Walker was born in 1852 at Steubenville, Ohio. At 11, his family moved to California. He worked his uncle's ranch near Lodi, then became a printer, plying his trade in Stockton and San Francisco. He was converted in 1872 during a Holiness meeting conducted by Methodists John Inskip and William McDonald, patriarchs in the American Holiness Movement. Walker joined a Methodist church, was called to preach, and entered the itinerant ministry, pastoring Methodist Episcopal churches in Santa Cruz, Pescadero, Crescent City, Lodi, Plano, and Ventura. At Santa Cruz, he met

Eliza Bennett, whom he married in 1875.

After Ventura, Walker transferred to the Presbyterian ministry and became pastor of San Francisco's Third Congregational Church. From there, he went to Virginia City, NV. Desiring more theological education, he moved his family to Pittsburgh, PA, where Walker studied two years at Western Theological Seminary. Afterward, he pastored Presbyterian congregations in Glenfield, PA; Martin's Ferry, OH; Evansville, IN; Parsons, KS; and Fort Collins, CO.

E. F. Walker

After his Fort Collins pastorate, Walker became a fulltime revivalist. The family home was established in Greencastle, IN. From this central base, Walker conducted revivals in every section of the nation. His slate was published regularly in *The Christian Witness*, the organ of the National Holiness Association, and he was a featured speaker at the General Holiness Convention of 1901 in Chicago, an interdenominational gathering that marked a high point in the Holiness Movement.

During much of his career, Walker belonged to the Indianapolis Presbytery. The family moved back to California in 1906, and in 1908, Walker transferred his credentials to the Pentecostal Church of the Nazarene, whose leaders he knew well. He pastored Pasadena First and Los Angeles First Churches, and edited until his death *The Pentecostal Bible Teacher*, the adult curriculum of the Church of the Nazarene. In 1899, Walker first published the book, *Sanctify Them: A Study of Our Lord's Prayer for His Disciples*. The book went through many editions, including several by the

New England District Assembly, 1912, with Walker presiding

Nazarene Publishing House. He also published *A Catechism for the Use of the Pentecostal Church of the Nazarene* in 1914.

Walker's general superintendency was memorable for two events. In 1914, he held a series of Holiness meetings in Scotland that helped cement the merger the following year between Nazarenes and the Pentecostal Church of Scotland.

Walker was also involved in events in 1916-17 that led to the withdrawal from the church of nearly 500 members under the leadership of Seth Rees. A contentious situation existed between Rees, the pastor of University Church in Pasadena, and the bulk of the district leadership. When the district superintendent disorganized University Church in order to deprive Rees of his base, a storm of controversy engulfed the infant denomination. Many saw this as the iron hand of episcopacy. Walker supported the action and was vilified by many for his stand. His colleagues on the Board of General Superintendents eventually forced him to publicly concede errors in procedure.

Walker, however, was held in greater esteem than ever by Bresee's coterie of disciples—C. J. Kinne, E. A. Girvin, and others—who regarded his support as essential for saving both the district and Pasadena College from disintegration. Following Walker's death on May 6, 1918, *Herald of Holiness* was flooded with tributes written by the Californians.

William C. Wilson

## William C. Wilson
### *The Fifth General Superintendent*

Early Nazarene history has tantalizing "what ifs?." What if E. P. Ellyson had not withdrawn from the general superintendency in 1911 after one term, or had not declined his reelection to it in 1915? What if W. C. Wilson had not died of preventable causes shortly after becoming general superintendent in 1915? Different circumstances or decisions could have recast the group of familiar leaders (Reynolds, Goodwin, Williams, and Chapman) who guided the church in the 1920s and 1930s.

William Columbus Wilson, the Church of the Nazarene's fifth general superintendent, was born December 22, 1866, in Hopkins County, KY. At 16, he was converted in a Methodist revival. He married Eliza Jones in 1886, joining the Missionary Baptist Church to which she (and his parents) belonged. Two years later, Wilson was sanctified and joined the Methodist Episcopal Church. He later told his son, Mallalieu, there was no sudden call to preach. He simply held prayer meetings and grew more active in ministry until there was a certainty that God wanted him to be a minister. He obeyed, sold his farm, and went to school.

In 1890, Wilson took the Greenville Circuit with three churches and organized a fourth. Then for two years, he served the Vine Grove Circuit with eight churches. His wife's sudden death during annual conference was a crushing blow. He was left with four young children.

W. C. Wilson, Alpin M. Bowes, and Bud Robinson, 1913

He became a revivalist, holding meetings in Kentucky and neighboring states. A stalwart in the Green River Holiness Association, Wilson preached alongside H. C. Morrison, L. L. Pickett, and other southern Holiness leaders. In 1896, he married school teacher Sarah Ragsdale. They met at a revival he conducted. Five children were born to this union.

Wilson was transferring his credentials to the M. E. Church, South when he was put on trial for violating southern Methodist discipline. He had conducted a holiness revival that competed with a local Methodist church's worship services. Discouraged, he considered launching a new Holiness church and briefly pastored an independent congregation. During this troubling time, C. W. Ruth wrote in August 1903, urging Wilson to join the Nazarenes, assuring him that "the Church of the Nazarene is nothing in the world but old-fashioned Methodism, with a Congregational form of government. Our business is to spread Scriptural Holiness over these lands." After reading a Nazarene *Manual*, Wilson agreed. He and his family united with Los Angeles First Church.

Wilson remained a revivalist until 1905, when the family moved to California. He pastored at Long Beach, Upland, and Pasadena First. From 1911-15, he was superintendent of the Southern California District. His relationship to Bresee was close, and in late 1914, Wilson presided over district assemblies in the Southeast in Bresee's stead.

The 1915 General Assembly elected Wilson general superintendent. He was probably Bresee's favored choice as successor. As someone who knew the Holiness Movement in both South and West, he could bridge fractious regional differences in the church. Indeed, after his election, Wilson made plans to move to Nashville to place a resident general superintendent in the South.

This was not to be. Bresee died a month after the Fourth General Assembly. Wilson was conducting the Dallas District Assembly when he learned of it. He proceeded to the San Antonio District Assembly, but left suddenly and returned home, feeling ill in his abdomen. His condition went up and down. Surgery on an ulcerated tooth left him with permanent headaches, and on December 19, he died.

The church was stunned. Relatively young and vigorous, Wilson was expected to play a crucial role in developing the church. Now he was gone.

He left behind his record of devotion as a founder, and he left a family that has given unbroken and unstinting service to the church ever since as pastors, educators, missionaries, and committed laity.

John W. Goodwin

## John W. Goodwin
### *The Sixth General Superintendent*

In his native Maine, John W. Goodwin was converted (1886), baptized, and entered the ministry (1890) through the influence of the Advent Christian Church, a product of the millenarian movement of the 1840s led by William Miller. Goodwin entered the ministry as a bi-vocational pastor, managing two departments in a shoe factory while serving a small church. This soon changed. He was ordained in 1893 and pastored Advent Christian churches in Maine, Massachusetts and New Hampshire until 1905.

John W. Goodwin

Increasingly he doubted Advent Christian positions on eschatology ("last things"). And by 1894, he was involved in interdenominational Holiness camp meetings across New England. He gradually accepted Methodist views of saving and sanctifying grace, the Church, and last things. Goodwin moved his family to California in 1905 and joined Los Angeles First Church of the Nazarene, which he had visited earlier.

He was quickly incorporated into Phineas Bresee's select inner circle, which included C. W. Ruth, E. A. Girvin, A. O. Henricks, C. J. Kinne, C. V. LaFontaine, H. Orton Wiley, Fred Epperson, and W. C. Wilson. With his dedicated work ethic and common sense, Goodwin emerged as one of Bresee's point men: founding pastor of Pasadena First Church, superintendent of the Southern California District, and business manager of Nazarene University. Goodwin's unceasing efforts spared Bresee's college from extinction during the gravest financial crisis of its early years.

J. B. Chapman perceived the Bresee-Goodwin relationship as close and personal, noting: "Bresee had many helpers, but, like Paul, only one son in the faith, and that son was John W. Goodwin."

Bresee's death just after the Fourth General Assembly (1915) was followed closely by that of General Superintendent W. C. Wilson. The district superintendents, by mail ballot, elected Goodwin (age 46) and R. T. Williams of Texas (age 32) to join H. F. Reynolds and E. F. Walker on the Board of General Superintendents. Goodwin and Williams remained colleagues for twenty-four and a half years, longer than any other pair of general superintendents. Williams noted in 1945 that they "did not always agree;" nevertheless, "our fellowship was never broken nor strained."

John Goodwin and family

Goodwin was involved in every momentous issue facing the church before 1940. He participated in a decision that, in 1917, rebuked a colleague, Walker, for approving the disorganization of the University Church in Pasadena during "the Seth Rees controversy." He shouldered heavy promotion work during various debt reduction campaigns of the 1910s and 1920s, including one to save the Nazarene Publishing House from financial collapse in 1922. He traveled constantly. Goodwin and Williams journeyed around the world together in 1929-30, conducting assemblies and meeting pastors and national workers in Japan, China, India, Palestine, Syria, Lebanon and Great Britain. Goodwin made other official visits to Mexico, Central and South America, and the British Isles. There was an unremitting round of annual district assemblies to conduct. He presided at hundreds of assemblies, ordaining nearly one thousand ministers, in an age before commercial aviation simplified travel and assemblies were shortened to a few days.

John W. Goodwin

John Goodwin retired from general office at the 1940 General Assembly. He spent his last years teaching homiletics at Pasadena College until his death in 1945.

## R. T. Williams
### *The Seventh General Superintendent*

R. T. Williams

R. T. Williams was ordained on the fifth day of the General Assembly at Pilot Point, Texas. As he knelt with fellow ordinands Emily Ellyson and Alpin Bowes, the hands of General Superintendent Hiram F. Reynolds touched Williams' head as he was set apart as an elder (full minister) "in the

The Board of General Superintendents in 1928, Goodwin, Reynolds, Williams, Chapman

Church of God" according to the procedures of the Pentecostal Church of the Nazarene. Reynolds' role as presiding elder in this ordination placed Williams in a succession of elders that trace back to Francis Asbury's ordination by Thomas Coke at the organizing conference of the Methodist Episcopal Church in 1784. Eight years after Pilot Point, Williams joined Reynolds as a general superintendent and presided at the ordination of hundreds of ministers over the next 30 years.

Roy T. Williams was born in Milam, TX in 1883 and raised in Many, Louisiana, 30 miles east of his birthplace. He was raised in a household that was not overtly religious, but, at 16, he attended a revival meeting at the New Hope Methodist Church and was converted. He was sanctified in the same revival. Josh Sanders, the visiting preacher, became Williams' pastor the next year.

R. T. Williams

In 1900, he entered Texas Holiness University. The college was located at Peniel, a community of Holiness people two miles from Greenville. The ministries of the Holiness Association of Texas were gathered there. These included the college, a camp meeting ground, a publishing company, and the Peniel Orphanage. Many evangelists lived there over the years, including Bud Robinson, Oscar Hudson, and E. C. DeJernett.

The school was led by President A. M. Hills, a graduate of Oberlin College and Yale Divinity School. Hills was a popular camp meeting and revival preacher who taught preaching to the ministerial students. He insisted that they should write out full sermon manuscripts. Williams hewed closely to Hills' advice for nearly a decade before shifting to sermon outlines. J. B. Chapman, who knew Williams for over 40 years, noted that the manuscript phase fostered in Williams logical thinking, accuracy, and mental discipline, so that he "preached well rather than excessively" and developed a reputation as a preacher of substance.

Goodwin and Williams

After graduation, Williams headed the small Bell City College for a time, but he soon returned to Peniel, where he taught English and psychology for several years. He and his wife joined the Nazarene congregation that P. F. Bresee organized there in early 1908, and he was ordained later that year at Pilot Point. In 1911, Williams followed E. P. Ellyson as the college's third president. He served for two years and then entered full-time revival work.

Two general superintendents died in late 1915—Phineas Bresee and W. C. Wilson. The district superintendents elected John Goodwin and R. T. Williams to fill these vacancies. Both were considered men of sound judgment, but Goodwin had broader pastoral and administrative experience, while Williams was the youngest person ever elected to the

office (before or since). Ironically, Williams' relative youth was a strong asset in the wake of the recent deaths and General Superintendent E. F. Walker's questionable health. He became a general superintendent at 32 and served in the office for 30 years, longer than any other person.

Goodwin once wrote that Williams was "a student of nature, a student of books, and a student of [people]." His stamina and judgment were needed greatly in the years ahead. Financial issues plagued the Church of the Nazarene for most of Williams' service as general superintendent, and he often became his board's "point man" in responding to this type of crisis. On various occasions, he worked to rally Nazarenes around the cause of saving the Nazarene Publishing House or one of the colleges from financial ruin. In the 1920s, he joined other leaders in reorganizing the church's general agencies by creating and then refining the General Board. In 1928, he delivered a notable address to the General Assembly on behalf of the Board of General Superintendents that lent support for a thorough revision of the church *Manual*.

R. T. Williams

H. F. Reynolds believed strongly that one or more general superintendents should visit the Nazarene churches around the world, as he had done in 1913-14. Williams and Goodwin were not convinced that this was necessary, but the 1928 General Assembly adopted Reynolds' point of view and directed that Williams and Goodwin visit the Nazarene work on other continents before the next assembly. They left in 1929, going first to Japan and China, then spending Christmas with the Rev. George Franklin and the missionaries in Kishorganj, in eastern India (now Bangladesh). From India, they went to Palestine and Syria. They kept the church informed of their progress through the pages of *Herald of Holiness* and *The Other Sheep,* and Williams wrote of this journey in greater detail in his book, *Glimpses Abroad*. A decade later, General Superintendent J. B. Chapman, accompanied by Maud, his wife, undertook a similar world tour.

Williams and Goodwin in China, circa 1929

Reynolds retired in 1932, and Goodwin and Williams were senior general superintendents until 1940, when Goodwin retired. War now raged in Europe and Asia, and Williams was the senior superintendent during the crucial war years.

Williams and his wife moved to a rural home near Tuscumbia, Missouri, near the Lake of the Ozarks. Haldor and Bertha Lillenas, whose daughter was married to their son, lived a short distance away. This rural retreat became a place where Williams could recover from the stress of constant travel.

R. T. Williams suffered a stroke in October 1945. He was incapacitated from that point until his death at his rural home in March 1946.

## Haldor and Bertha Lillenas
### *The Clergy Couple Who Birthed a Publishing Company*

Haldor and Bertha Lillenas

They are buried in Kansas City's Forest Hill Cemetery, a four-minute drive from Nazarene Theological Seminary and the former campus of the Nazarene international headquarters. Legendary baseball pitcher Satchel Paige's tomb and monument are about 35 yards north of their graves. A small hill, across a shady lane to their east, is the burial place of Confederate veterans and their families, including General Jo Shelby, while many African-Americans are buried just west of their gravesites.

He was an immigrant, born in Norway. She was a native of Kentucky. Their lives intersected and joined in Pasadena, California. A simple tombstone bears the immigrant's surname: "Lillenas." Footstones add details. One is inscribed: "Father & Husband, Haldor Lillenas, Hymn Writer. 1885-1959." The other says: "Wife & Mother, Bertha Mae Lillenas, Hymn Writer. 1889-1945."

Bertha Lillenas

The name is well-known to those raised in the Church of the Nazarene before 1970, and "Lillenas Publishing Company" has been imprinted on music published by the Nazarene Publishing House since 1930. Haldor and Bertha Lillenas were a clergy-couple. Our tale hangs on that fact.

Bertha was the second child of W. C. Wilson, a Methodist pastor and evangelist. Her mother died in 1893. She and her three siblings were placed with different relatives while their father, distraught and unable to raise them alone, regained his bearings. Wilson remarried two years later, and the children were gradually reunited in the home their new stepmother provided. The family also grew, as four other children were born to Wilson and his second wife.

Haldor Lillenas

W. C. Wilson joined the Church of the Nazarene in 1905, after an appeal from C. W. Ruth, who assured him that the Nazarenes represented a democratic form of "old-fashioned Methodism." A few months later, the family left Kentucky for California, where W. C. Wilson eventually secured a place as one of Phineas Bresee's right-hand men, serving as pastor of key churches and as superintendent of the Southern California District. In 1906, Bertha joined her brother Guy as a student at Deets Bible College, the small Nazarene school in Los Angeles that would grow into Pasadena College (now Point Loma Nazarene University).

There Bertha met Haldor Lillenas, a young Norwegian born on an island south of Bergen. His family immigrated to America when Haldor was two, moving during his childhood from the Dakotas to Oregon, then

back east to Minnesota. At 21, Haldor returned to Astoria, OR, the place of many cherished memories. In 1906, he came into contact with the Peniel Mission there and experienced an evangelical conversion. He joined the Nazarenes soon afterward and moved to Los Angeles to attend Deets Bible College.

Haldor Lillenas

Haldor and Bertha met through one of the college's many traveling music groups. Her contralto and his tenor complimented one another. They married in 1910 and formed a talented team. Both preached, sang, and composed songs. Their careers alternated between co-pastorates and periods of full-time evangelism, but in whatever field of service they were in, they shared the preaching and music responsibilities.

Their first ministry together was at the Peniel Mission in Sacramento, which they led for one year. Then they co-pastored the Nazarene church at Lompoc, CA, from 1911-12. Both were ordained by General Superintendent H. F. Reynolds at the 1912 assembly of the Southern California District. They subsequently co-pastored at Pomona, CA (1912-14), Auburn, IL (1916-19), Peniel, TX (1919-20), and Redlands, CA (1920-23). The most pivotal pastorate of their career, though, proved to be Indianapolis First Church of the Nazarene.

They served as the congregation's pastors from 1923-26. The membership grew from 150 to 250 during their tenure. During these

Haldor Lillenas at the piano with singers at the 1940 General Assembly

Haldor Lillenas with a Peniel Mission Group, 1906

years, Bertha Lillenas' sermon, "Christian Freedom," was published in *The Nazarene Pulpit,* an anthology that showcased Nazarene preaching. Her brother, Mallalieu Wilson, states that during this pastorate, "as Haldor gave increasing attention to music, Bertha took more of the preaching responsibility."

Indeed, Haldor dreamed of heading his own music publishing company, and in 1926 they resigned. Bertha began conducting revivals, assisted by Haldor when he could, but his energies were now focused on launching a successful Christian music business.

The Lillenas Publishing Company's success depended on Haldor's talent and enterprise, but it also succeeded partly because of his unique marriage—a true anomaly of its day. American women of that time, even those with college degrees, typically enjoyed careers only if they remained single. Those who married invariably gave them up. Nazarene clergy women were among the few exceptions. Bertha Lillenas' career was a key element in her husband's ability to put wings under his dream. The financial contributions she made served as the family's financial buffer as the Lillenas Publishing Company made its way through the rocky early years of its existence.

Haldor and Bertha in Kansas City with daughter Evangeline and son-in-law Reginald Williams

It was not an easy go, but it proved successful. The Nazarene Publishing House in Kansas City noticed. It wanted to improve its music program under the leadership of someone with a proven track record, and in 1930, it offered to buy the Lillenas Publishing Company as a subsidiary and retain Haldor as its manager. The offer ensured the company's survival and fit the Lillenases' notion of churchmanship. They accepted the offer and moved to Kansas City.

Evangeline Williams and Bertha Lillenas

For the remainder of their marriage, they worked on music together and often traveled, promoting the product of the music company that bore their name.

Bertha's health declined in the late 1930s. In about 1940, they moved to "Melody Lane," a stone house that they built in central Missouri, near the Lake of the Ozarks. Haldor visited the publishing house in Kansas City one day a week for meetings, but composed and edited music in his home office. Bertha assisted on many of his projects, and her death in 1945 ended a wonderful partnership of 35 years.

After Bertha's death, Haldor married Lola Kellogg, a nurse. They traveled extensively together. He died in 1959 in a car accident in Aspen, Colorado.

Haldor with Lola Kellogg

### Hiroshi Kitagawa
### *Bearing the Cross of Leadership*

Hiroshi Kitagawa left behind many of the Nazarene footprints in Japan. He was born in Kumamoto in 1888. His father and older brother were converts to the Russian Orthodox Church. This embarrassed young Hiroshi, who felt a keen sense of social stigma over their adherence to a minority religion in their predominantly Buddhist area. He kept Christianity at arm's length throughout his childhood.

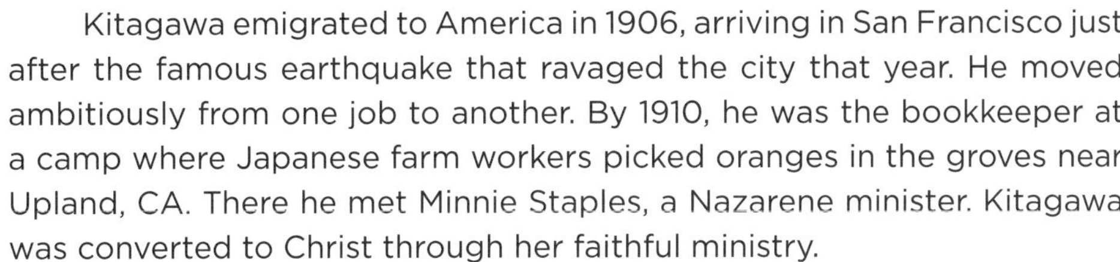

Kitagawa emigrated to America in 1906, arriving in San Francisco just after the famous earthquake that ravaged the city that year. He moved ambitiously from one job to another. By 1910, he was the bookkeeper at a camp where Japanese farm workers picked oranges in the groves near Upland, CA. There he met Minnie Staples, a Nazarene minister. Kitagawa was converted to Christ through her faithful ministry.

Hiroshi Kitagawa

He entered Nazarene University in Pasadena. There, he met many of the church's early leaders and was drawn fully into Nazarene life. He and Staples also ministered to the Japanese living in Los Angeles. Nobumi Isayama was converted through this ministry. Kitagawa also met William Eckel, son of the Southern California District's superintendent. These were crucial connections. In a few short years, Kitagawa, Isayama, Staples, and Eckel were working shoulder-to-shoulder in Japan.

Kitagawa graduated in 1914 and was ordained by Phineas Bresee a few weeks later. He returned to Japan the next year in the company of Staples and her husband. Together, they began evangelizing in Kumamoto. Through their joint efforts, the first organized Nazarene church in Japan was established. Kitagawa became its first pastor. His younger brother, Shiro Kitagawa, was one of the first members.

Hiroshi Kitagawa Family

While Minnie Staples turned her attention to evangelizing across the island of Kyushu, Kitagawa concentrated on strengthening the Kumamoto church and providing theological education to the growing number who professed a call to preach. Within a year of his return to Japan, Kitagawa also headed a Bible school. Still later, he added the responsibility of publishing the Nazarene paper, *Heavenly Way*.

Hiroshi Kitagawa Family

These successes prepared him to assume a prominent place in the development of the church in Japan. In 1922, J. I. Nagamatsu was elected as the first national district superintendent, but resigned a few months later to go to America. Kitagawa—now pastor of the Honmachi Church of the Nazarene in Kyoto, where the Bible school had also moved—succeeded Nagamatsu and juggled the roles of pastor, educator, and district superintendent until 1935, when his brother Shiro took up the district responsibility.

World War II took a heavy toll on Japanese Nazarenes. The government forced Japan's Protestants to unite into one body that obliterated denominational distinctions. Nazarene pastors were conscripted into the military and some died in other lands. American bombs destroyed over half of the country's Nazarene church buildings. Kitagawa and his wife starved in the war's waning days, and until their son returned home to provide for them, faced the genuine threat of a slow death .

The Church of the Nazarene in Japan had to be reorganized in the war's aftermath. Once again, Hiroshi Kitagawa was involved. His church in Kyoto was the site where the surviving Nazarene pastors met with missionary William Eckel in 1947 to plan the rebuilding of the Nazarene vineyard. Leadership was passing into younger hands, but Kitagawa continued to serve. His last pastorate was in Yokohama, where he died in 1975.

Robert Balie Mitchum

**Robert Balie Mitchum**
***The Value of a Consecrated Layman***

Nazarene lay people have participated in the church's work by the hundreds of thousands, volunteering time, abilities, and resources. Robert Balie Mitchum's exemplary service illustrates the ethic of lay ministry that characterizes the Wesleyan tradition, and Nazarene life, at its best.

A Baptist, Mitchum married Donie Adams, a staunch Methodist whose brothers included two circuit-riding preachers. They had four children. He owned a general store in Milan, TN, served on the school board, and was

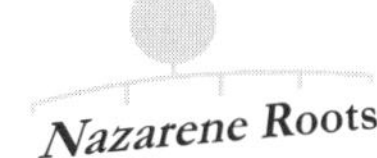


a Baptist deacon. Donie remained an active Methodist.

Their lives were altered when evangelist Robert Lee Harris held a revival in Milan in 1893 at Donie's invitation. A bond grew between the evangelist and R. B. Mitchum, who opened his home to Harris and his wife, Mary, as a base for their ministry in west Tennessee. The Mitchum boys set the type for Harris' modest paper, *The Trumpet,* in the basement. When Harris organized a Holiness church in Milan in July 1894, the Mitchums were charter members.

Mitchums, Sheekses, and Mary Lee Cagle, surviving charter members of the Milan, TN, Church

Harris died of tuberculosis in November and was buried in the Mitchum family plot. His church should have died, too, but its lay members were committed to its future. Donie Mitchum and Mary Harris began preaching in Milan, then broadened their activities to conducting area revivals with another woman, Elliott Sheeks. New congregations formed.

R. B. Mitchum, busy with his store, remained the pillar of the Milan church. He gave sound counsel and financial support to the women, participating in their meetings as time permitted. He defended their ministry against those who attacked its scriptural validity. As churches multiplied, he was a leading voice at the New Testament Church of Christ's first general council in 1899, where Mary Harris and Elliott Sheeks were ordained. By then, Mary Harris ministered largely in Texas, where she soon married H. C. Cagle. Elliott Sheeks' ministry focused on Arkansas. For several years, Donie Mitchum preached across northwest Tennessee.

Then financial misfortune struck. R. B. Mitchum lost his store. His new job required travel, and he and Donie reversed ministry roles. She became the family anchor at home and the mainstay of the Milan church; he became the Barnabas who visited the connection's churches across west Tennessee while traveling on business.

They moved to Nashville in 1905, and R. B. Mitchum built a successful delivery business. The family prospered and purchased a large home where they entertained itinerant preachers and others, and provided a home to a Hindu convert from India, Beecher Ashton.

R. B. Mitchum's involvement in church matters never abated. He forged links to other Holiness people in Nashville, including the Pentecostal

Mission. He participated in the merger of southern groups that created the Holiness Church of Christ in 1904. And he served as president of that denomination at the time of its merger with the Pentecostal Church of the Nazarene at Pilot Point, TX, in 1908.

He served on the General Boards of Foreign Missions (1911-15, 1919-23) and Church Extension (1915-19) and was elected to the General Board upon its creation in 1923, which he served on continuously until 1936, representing the southeast United States. He was a member of its Department of Foreign Missions throughout and was its liaison on the General Board Finance Committee. He was a delegate to every General Assembly from 1908 to 1932, save one. Equally involved in local and district affairs, Mitchum was the church treasurer and a Sunday school teacher at Nashville Grace Church for many years.

R. B. Mitchum died in Nashville in 1937 and was buried in Milan beside R. L. Harris. His influence lives on in the General Board and in the Church of the Nazarene's international spread.

## Bud Robinson
### *The Education of an Evangelist*

Bud Robinson

Bud Robinson was among the unlikeliest persons ever called to preach. Illiterate, subject at one stage in life to epileptic fits, and afflicted with a severe stutter, he had known nothing but poverty. Yet, each limitation eventually was overcome. He became the Church of the Nazarene's best-loved evangelist and columnist, an author, a dedicated promoter of the Nazarene Publishing House and *Herald of Holiness*, and a lover of Nazarene colleges.

He was born in 1860 in White County, Tennessee, one of thirteen children born into a destitute family that had once known better times. His father returned from the Civil War and moved the family to Mississippi in a vain attempt to improve their fortunes. They retreated, several years later and, no richer, back to Tennessee's Cumberland Mountains.

His father's death left the widow Robinson with 10 children still to raise. In 1876, she moved her family to Dallas County, Texas. Bud worked as a farm and ranch hand. Like the typical cowboy, he was a "dirt-poor" southern youth.

In 1880, an itinerant Methodist preacher impressed him, and Bud attended a camp meeting that August, where he was converted. He often said later that he "got religion in the old-fashioned shouting Methodist manner." The very night of his conversion, the conviction began to grow within him that he was called to preach.

The education of Bud Robinson began, born of an earnest desire to answer that call. He obtained a New Testament and began teaching himself to read. At age 56, he remembered: "When I was saved, my heart so longed for an education that I lay on my face with my Bible before me by day and by night." It was the only book he owned for a long time. He studied it so thoroughly that later he could claim: "I have rarely heard a man take a text or read a chapter for years but what I knew the text or chapter by heart."

Bud Robinson

Robinson applied for a Methodist preacher's license. His speech impediment and lack of education led the conference to reject his application, but they reconsidered, relented, and licensed him. No area preacher would invite him to hold a service at first, so on Saturdays, he preached to whatever crowd he could gather. Two years passed before he began receiving regular calls to preach from area pulpits.

In 1890, he testified to the grace of entire sanctification. His education continued apace. He later wrote: "As the great Holiness movement swept on, they began to send out good books, and as they came from the press, I bought and read and reread them. As others would be printed, I would grab them and almost devour them. I can say that I have read good books by the hundreds."

Bud Robinson on his porch in Texas

His ministry expanded across Texas, the South, and finally the United States. More and more channels opened for service, including the Holiness Association of Texas and the National Holiness Association. In 1908, he united with the fledgling Pentecostal Church of the Nazarene.

Uncle Buddy Robinson and friends, 1933

His revivals became noticed in virtually every community where he conducted them. Southern idiom and masterful use of the storyteller's art became his stock in trade. When he preached, a lisp was the only remaining trace of his one-time stutter. A 1906 headline in the Atlanta *Constitution* noted his impact in that city: "Weeping Men and Women Fell at Preacher's Feet; More Than Two Hundred People Rushed to the Platform When 'Bud' Robinson Called 'Come to the Front.'"

Bud Robinson

He began writing a weekly column that eventually was published in several Holiness papers. In *Herald of Holiness,* it was titled "Uncle Buddy's Good Samaritan Chats." Newsy in content, the column reflected his many friendships and associations across Methodist, Nazarene, Pilgrim Holiness, and Salvation Army boundaries, reminding readers of all denominations that they were workers together in the Lord's vineyard.

Whether conducting "Coast to Coast" revivals with Methodist evangelist Will Huff or preaching at a district camp meeting, Bud Robinson always remained approachable, down to earth, and genuine, even at the height of his career.

He believed strongly in the Holiness press and was noted for selling subscriptions to *Herald of Holiness.* He was equally zealous for Holiness colleges. At Peniel, a Holiness enclave near Greenville, Texas, the spacious home he and his wife, Sally, maintained for a decade provided free lodging to ministerial students attending Texas Holiness University. Later in life, he became a fixture at commencement exercises at various Nazarene colleges, including Olivet, where home movies from the 1930s show him walking good naturedly in cap and gown.

Bud Robinson

In 1916, he wrote: "All that I have done has been done at a great disadvantage; and if I were not too old today, I would start in now and go to school for four or five years. If I could drop back about sixteen years, and that would make me forty, I would take five years to get a good education."

Bud Robinson died in Pasadena, California, in 1942, where he lived from 1912 on. His ministry, a biographer noted, was a "miracle of grace."

E. P. Ellyson

## E. P. Ellyson
### *The Nazarene Sunday School*

Sunday schools have always been important to Nazarenes as a means of outreach, Christian nurture, and Biblical education.

The People's Church of Providence, RI, our oldest congregation, set up Sunday School classes and elected a superintendent to guide them soon after its founding in 1887. A Sunday School Committee of nine was appointed. Their duties: approve books for the church library, keep Sunday School records, visit church and Sunday School-related families, visit those "in the community [who] neglect the house of God," and welcome strangers. The superintendent and church librarian were *ex*

*officio* members of this committee.

When Los Angeles First Church was founded eight years later and a continent away, a church school program developed there as Bresee drew upon his experience as a Methodist pastor. Rev. Lucy Knott edited a Sunday School column in *The Nazarene Messenger* for many years.

In 1905, the Nazarene Publishing Company of Los Angeles began marketing Pentecostal Sunday School Literature, a curriculum published in Louisville, KY, by the Pentecostal Publishing Company, a major Holiness publisher. John Paul, a Methodist, was general editor of the line. The southern Holiness Church of Christ was using the same curriculum by 1907, when the Nazarene Publishing Company purchased the rights to publish it. The transfer of these rights marks the real beginning of systematic Nazarene curriculum.

The Pentecostal Sunday School curriculum moved to Kansas City in 1912 after the general assembly authorized a central publishing house. Today's Nazarene Publishing House curriculum descends from that early curriculum published in Louisville and Los Angeles. The curriculum's early Nazarene writers and editors included E. F. Walker, E. P. Ellyson, Emily Ellyson, and C. E. Cornell.

The 1923 General Assembly took action to raise the profile of the Sunday School interests. It authorized a Department of Church Schools for the denomination and elected E. P. Ellyson to head it. Ellyson had served a single term as general superintendent from 1908 to 1911 and was

E. P. Ellyson at Peniel University in Texas

E. P. Ellyson and Mary Emily Ellyson in Pasadena

E. P. Ellyson with Japanese students at Nazarene University in Pasadena

E. P. Ellyson and
R. T. Williams in Texas

re-elected to that office in 1915, but declined. However, he accepted his election to this new department, for he saw it as an extension of his long-time ministry in higher education. He brought prestige and competence to a new leadership position that he held for the next 17 years. As his chief assistant, he hired his wife, Rev. Mary Emily Ellyson, who had taught on the religion faculty of several Nazarene colleges. And he utilized a wide range of previously untapped talent, including Olive Winchester, a New Testament professor at Northwest Nazarene College, who was a graduate of the prestigious Radcliffe College and the University of Glasgow.

The Nazarene Sunday School has shaped disciples young and old, molding Christian identity, teaching theology, and instilling purpose. During the Mid-Century Crusade for Souls, the Sunday School was seen principally as an evangelistic tool. In other periods, it has been regarded as a potent force for teaching the Bible and creating a sense of Christian community. And it has reflected some of each aspect in all periods.

**E. E. Angell**
***Higher Education***

E. E. Angell

Rev. Ernest E. Angell was a Methodist by lineage, a Congregationalist by choice, and finally a Pentecostal Nazarene. He represented the best aspirations of the early Nazarenes of the northeastern United States.

Born in New York State in 1875, Angell graduated in 1900 from Wesleyan Theological College, an affiliated institution of McGill University in Montreal. He was the pastor of Congregational churches in East Barre and Orange, VT, when he came under the influence of Laura Gale, a member of an independent Holiness church in Lowell, MA. She aided him in the spiritual deepening that resulted in his profession of entire sanctification in 1901. The following year, he married Gale's daughter, Bertha, and that summer became pastor of the Pentecostal Church at Saratoga Springs, NY. Later, he was pastor of the John Wesley Church in Brooklyn. By 1906, he was an active and respected member of the Association of Pentecostal Churches of America, and in that year, he agreed to head its Pentecostal Collegiate Institute in North Scituate, RI.

As institute president and a member of the Association of Pentecostal Churches' standing Missionary Committee, Angell played a central role in the union of the eastern Holiness churches with those of the west coast led by Phineas Bresee. While travelling upriver on a steamer with

Rev. C. W. Ruth, assistant general superintendent of the Church of the Nazarene, Angell conferred at length on the possibility of a church union. He introduced Ruth to the Missionary Committee when it next met. This proved to be a significant event paving the way for the union of the two bodies in Chicago the following year. Angell exerted influence on the educational policy of the new Pentecostal Church of the Nazarene, serving as secretary of the early General Assembly Education Committees.

Angell in 1907 in Chicago

Until 1913, Angell remained president of PCI, developing its faculty and program, and adding a manual labor emphasis to the institution. Seeking relief from a crushing burden of administration, Angell resigned and recuperated for a period before accepting the pastorate of the Richmond Hill, NY church in 1915. Three years later, he was elected district superintendent of the New York District, serving until 1922, when he returned to the college now known as Eastern Nazarene College and located in Wollaston, MA. At ENC, he accepted the dual assignment of pastor of the college church and dean of the theology department. With one foot in the parish and the other in academic life, Angell pressed his vision of the Christian life as one that joined grace and spirit with mind and life. Dr. Samuel Young later stated that E.E. Angell "was a Christian mystic. . . . living for the unseen things." Young added: "He loved the church—the whole church—and was interested in her every problem. He was never provincial in his outlook."

In 1936, Angell went west to become dean of theology at Northwest Nazarene College in Nampa, Idaho. He died there three years later.

E. E. Angell in academic regalia, 1925

Angell was a true native son of his region and represented the concern of the eastern Nazarenes to establish and maintain a high educational tone within religious life. At a wider level, Angell represented a distinct type of well-rounded life that found its completeness through a combination of parish, district, and educational experiences.

### Theodore and Minnie Ludwig
### *The Challenge of Evangelism*

Revivals and evangelism were dominant threads in the fabric of early Nazarene life. Phineas Bresee envisioned the Nazarene movement as a network of urban "centers of holy fire" spanning North America. Hiram F. Reynolds, from a different angle of vision, called the church to assume a role in world evangelization. The visions cast by these leaders differed,

Theodore Ludwig

Minnie Brink Ludwig

but evangelism, central in both viewpoints, ultimately links them. And Theodore and Minnie Ludwig were among those whose lives moved to the rhythm of this evangelistic impulse.

Theodore Ludwig was raised among German-Americans in Illinois. He was six and a half years old when the Salem German Methodist Episcopal Church was erected on his father's farm. It proved a sound investment of time and resources. Ludwig later noted that "in this Salem Church, all of the 11 children [of my parents] were saved in childhood or early youth. I, Theo, was saved at the age of 10-years in a revival, Oct. 1880."

He graduated from Central Wesleyan College, Warrensburg, MO, and studied for one year at Garrett Biblical Institute near Chicago. Bishop Stephen Merrill ordained him in 1902, and Ludwig's early ministry was in Illinois and Missouri to German-speaking churches of the St. Louis Conference, including the Salem church of his youth. During the Salem pastorate, his son, Sylvester Theodore, was born (1903) and baptized as an infant in the very church where the father had first professed his Christian faith. But this early ministry was marked also by tragedy. Ludwig's first wife died in 1905, leaving the busy pastor alone, with a small child to raise.

Minnie Brink, meanwhile, was born in 1877 in Nashville, IL. She was converted just before age 20 in St. Louis. She testified to the grace of entire sanctification the next year at a southern Illinois camp meeting. She worked for several years at the Lighthouse Mission in St. Louis, serving two years as a city missionary and sharing the gospel with people in their homes. The Free Methodist Church licensed her to preach in 1904, and she spent a year conducting revivals with Blanche Smith. St. Louis friends introduced her to Theodore Ludwig, then a pastor in Cape Girardeau, MO. They married in 1906. A few weeks after their wedding, Theo was led into the grace of entire sanctification through Minnie's influence.

Minnie Ludwig devoted several years to raising Sylvester and assisting Theo's ministry. They jointly conducted occasional revivals in nearby churches. In 1908, Theodore was appointed to a German Methodist church in Boody, IL. There, a layman gave them copies of *The Christian Witness,* the weekly paper of the National Holiness Association. Their knowledge of the wider Holiness Movement grew, as did their contacts within it.

Impressed by reports about C. E. Cornell and Chicago First Church of the Nazarene, they secured and studied a Nazarene *Manual*. H. F. Reynolds received them into the Church of the Nazarene in 1912 at Hastings, NE, and they pastored home mission churches at Kennesaw and York, NE, for the next few years.

In 1914, Phineas Bresee ordained Minnie Ludwig at the Nebraska District Assembly. This soon led to a turning point: for the next 40 years the Ludwigs devoted their energies to public evangelism, conducting revivals in 40 states and in Canada.

Theo and Minnie Ludwig

Revival meetings were typically two or three weeks long. The Ludwigs shared the preaching. It was estimated near the end of their lives that Minnie and Theodore had preached over 8,000 and 9,000 sermons respectively.

Evangelist C. T. Corbett noted their contrasting personalities and styles. Theodore was a teacher-preacher, while Minnie "was of the more fervent type. As a stirring preacher, she plowed deeply into the soul need of the people. . . . She usually dressed in white, being very feminine, yet forceful in her delivery. Together, they lifted up a Christ that could save."

The Brink family, Minnie Ludwig's birth family. She is standing center left.

Theo Ludwig provided leadership as president of the denomination's General Orphanage Board and as superintendent of the Nebraska and Southeast Atlantic Districts. Yet, evangelism remained the heartbeat of their ministry. While he was D.S. in Nebraska, she was the district evangelist, and they planted 16 churches across the state in three years. Their son wrote that "the burdens of administration were always secondary to the primary task of winning souls." The "method was simple. He and Minnie would pitch a tent or rent a store building and begin a meeting, often staying until a church was organized." In Broadwater, NE, they preached nightly for five weeks, organizing a 75-member church at the conclusion of the meeting.

S. T. Ludwig, general secretary

They likewise used the printed word to reach people. Theodore Ludwig's *The Life of Victory* (1929) had a simple structure: "How to Get and Keep Saved" and "How to Obtain and Retain Entire Sanctification." Minnie Ludwig's *His Guiding Hand* (1941) was a narrative of her Christian experience and call to the ministry. Her best-known book, *At the Crossroads* (1928), drew, as did their other books, upon a reservoir of varied experiences in ministry.

Theodore Ludwig rejoiced in many things in later life: the creation of Nazarene Theological Seminary ("I've been praying for this for years"), the "Showers of Blessing" radio broadcast, and in his son, S. T. Ludwig, president of Bresee College in the 1930s and the denomination's general secretary from 1948 to 1964. Theodore Ludwig died in 1957. Minnie Ludwig died the following year. They are buried near her childhood home in Nashville, IL.

**J. B. Chapman**
***The Advocate of Graduate Theological Education***

J. B. Chapman

J. B. Chapman initiated the first decade of instruction at Nazarene Theological Seminary in a wide-ranging convocation address designed to foster the notion that theology was dynamic and universal, not rigid and provincial. His own views were no doubt influenced by A.M. Hills, president of Texas Holiness University during the years that Chapman emerged as a young, regional Holiness leader. In turn, Hills was a product of Oberlin College, where Charles Finney and Asa Mahan recast Calvinist theology in a perfectionist light, and of Yale, where the New Divinity of Nathanial Taylor had turned arid Calvinist apologetics toward respect for revivalistic evangelicalism.

Hills' views, though fixed, implicitly recognized the changing nature of theology. The content of his two-volume *Fundamental Christian Theology*, published in 1931, differed markedly from the theology texts from which he had learned the elements of Christian doctrine. Similarly, H. Orton Wiley framed a different vision of the theological task in his three-volume *Christian Theology,* published a decade after Hills' opus. In the succession from Oberlin perfectionism to Hills' systematic to Wiley's, there is discernible movement from Finney's theological agenda toward John Wesley's. The theologians differed on content and form, but their perspectives all hung together as perfectionist theologies intent on relating sanctification to human life.

J. B. Chapman when he first began to preach

Chapman's convocation address to the Nazarene seminary community stated the essential point: "Doctrine is not a goal within itself. The goal is God and right relations to Him and state before Him. But doctrine is like a highway that leads to the goal."

Such issues were not new to Chapman, who became involved in Nazarene higher education at an early point in his career, serving as theology professor at Peniel College in Texas and as president of Arkansas Holiness College.

He understood that Nazarene colleges, even from their origins, were caught between impulses that often clashed: sectarian purpose and broader Christian ideals. The point is illustrated by a statement in 1902

announcing the founding of Pacific Bible College in Pasadena, CA, the forerunner of present-day Point Loma Nazarene University: "For some time, this work has been pressed upon us; to open a school that should teach the *Word*, with such collateral courses of history and Christian work." Though the school was to be operated under the control of the Church of the Nazarene, the announcement claimed that "this college is not sectarian, but is in the broad sense Christian. . . . It seeks not sectarianism, but Bible culture for all men and women who may desire to avail themselves of its advantages."

Still, sectarianism could hardly be avoided. In 1917, the college at Pasadena was at the center of a struggle between competing elements of the Southern California District that resulted in a small but significant schism known as the "Rees Dissension." The Nazarene college could no more separate itself from sectarian concerns than could the denomination that supported it. Indeed, the larger history of Nazarene higher education has often been shaped by the same tension between sectarian purpose and broader Christian ideals that gave rise to the schools themselves.

In the 1920s, Chapman and H. Orton Wiley led the way in urging a strong system of liberal arts colleges across the church. Sometimes they faced detractors who considered this an unnecessary direction to take "for the training of ministers," but they argued that an intelligent and educated Christian laity was just as essential as an educated ministry if the church was to achieve its social and religious goals.

Chapman articulated the broader view behind a liberal arts college in 1930 when he dedicated Fowler Memorial Building on the Eastern Nazarene College campus. Citing St. Paul's statement to early Christians that "all things are yours" (1 Corinthians 3:21), Chapman argued that "the treasures of art and literature belong to the Christian and the Church." Though some of his thoughts showed affinity with the period's fundamentalism, Chapman was direct in declaring that "there is no war between science and Christianity," adding, "We are bound to accept the demonstrated facts of science, even though they may upset theories and shade time-honored creeds." He paid further tribute to the nonsectarian ideal by noting that the building he was dedicating was named in honor of Rev. C.J. Fowler, whom his immediate audience knew well was a Methodist, not a Nazarene.

His lifetime concern for sound education led Chapman to advocate on behalf of a graduate school of theology for the Nazarenes as far back as 1926. His dream did not come true until 1945, when Nazarene Theological Seminary opened.

> "The great men of the Holiness movement have been scholars and seminary men; like John Wesley, Adam Clarke, John Fletcher, Joseph Benson, [Amos] Binney, Daniel Steele . . . That there have been many effective preachers who were not well educated in the schools is largely creditable to the fact that the educated ones worked out our theses so well and defended our tenets so well that the others were able to project our doctrines in confidence."

Olivet College Worship

The seminary was not welcomed by all, but Chapman stoutly defended its value against critics. His response to one critic is instructive. He began:

"Where the idea [originated] that Holiness people do not believe in education . . . is a mystery. [Those] who believe that God works His sovereign will without the consent of the human will may well think of education as non-essential. But for people like us, who hold that element of intelligent cooperation with God is essential from the very beginning and even to the end of the Christian course, there is no escape from the necessity of education. And the great men of the Holiness Movement have been scholars and seminary men; like John Wesley, Adam Clarke, John Fletcher, Joseph Benson, Binney, Daniel Steele, Asbury Lowery, etc. That there have been many effective preachers who were not well-educated in the schools is largely creditable to the fact that the educated ones worked out our theses so well and defended out tenets so well that the others were able to project our doctrines in confidence. . . . I do not think you will find

"The revival I seek is not the product of the labors of some personality-plus evangelist. Such a revival is too detached and impersonal to meet my needs or to answer my prayers. I want that kind of revival that comes in spite of the singing, the preaching, the testimonies, and the human attractions . . . it takes that kind to really revive me."

A group of Peniel College boys

J. B. Chapman leading devotions at the Nazarene Headquarters in Kansas City

J. B. Chapman

in the annals of Christianity any instances of where God overlooked the necessity for human training before entrance into successful propagation of the gospel."

Was it not the case, Chapman's correspondent wrote, that "Uncle Buddy" Robinson was a successful worker in the Kingdom without seminary education? "If you are familiar with the life of Bud Robinson," Chapman replied, "you know that he served an apprenticeship of twenty years after his conversion before he actually became effective in his work . . . and is not an exception at all; he might have made it quicker with the help of schools."

Chapman then testified, "I cannot speak for the other general superintendents, but my own story is this: I was called to the ministry and began to preach at 16. Later, I finished college with an A.B., stayed on two years for the theological course and received a B.D., and then spent six years teaching Philosophy, Theism, and Christian Evidences. . . . And all I can say, if I had it to do again, is that I would try to get better training than I did. I believe our Seminary is a necessary step in the forward program of our church, and my interest in it is exactly like my interest on any other branch of the church—souls and the Kingdom's increase."

"We tried the grammar and high schools and the Bible school, but we have settled on the college as the best sector of the educational processes for the purpose of general culture."

H. Orton Wiley

**H. Orton Wiley**
***Theologian and Educator***

H. Orton Wiley was the church's most significant 20th-century theologian. He was born in Nebraska and lived briefly there and in Oregon, but he was raised mainly in northern California. The United Brethren in Christ, a German Methodist church, was the cradle of his early Christian faith. He was studious and earned his first two degrees in teaching and pharmacy.

In 1901, he moved to Berkeley, California, and entered the United Brethren ministry the following year. He grew acquainted with a Nazarene pastor, E. A. Girvin, who influenced his decision to unite with the Nazarenes. Phineas Bresee ordained him in 1906, and Wiley earned a ministerial degree in 1910 from Pacific Theological Seminary (now Pacific School of Theology) in Berkeley. Bresee then invited Wiley to Pasadena, CA, to be vice-president of Nazarene University and dean of Deets Pacific Bible School. Wiley served throughout E. P. Ellyson's administration (1911-13) and became the school's third president when Ellyson left.

A. J. Ramsey

Wiley's first presidency of Pasadena College ended badly, for he aligned himself with Seth Rees in a controversy that engulfed the district. Wiley brought Professor A. J. Ramsey to Pasadena to succeed him as dean of the school of theology. Ramsey forged a close friendship with W. C. Wilson. However, Rees and his associates eventually attacked Ramsey, insisting that he was "not a true holiness man." Ramsey was vindicated, but resigned in disillusionment with the Nazarenes. Wiley's alliance with Rees cost him his job at this time, so Wiley returned to Berkeley to work on a doctorate. Back in Pasadena, A. M. Hills replaced Ramsey as dean of theology, but Rees' people now attacked Hills, claiming that he also was "not a true holiness man." Eventually Rees and several hundred people left the Church of the Nazarene. The following year, after Wiley became president of Northwest Nazarene College, Rees and his allies interfered with the school there, and Wiley's attitude toward Rees changed. Wiley learned from his mistakes and grew in his understanding of people and of the forces inside and outside the colleges that shaped the educational environment.

H. Orton Wiley, as a young graduate

Over his career, Wiley made major contributions to the church in two areas: higher education and theology. In education, he was the founding president of Northwest Nazarene College, and he served three times as

president of Pasadena College. He also worked closely with J. B. Chapman in shaping denomination-wide educational policy.

Wiley's influence on Nazarene theology was evident by the 1920s. He served on the *Manual* editing committee from 1919 to 1932, and Ross Price, a student and later a colleague, noted that Wiley "was always consulted by the committee on any matters relating to either our doctrine or our faith." His theological influence was evident at the 1928 General Assembly, when the Articles of Faith were revised at several points, including the article on Scripture. In the mid-1920s, *Preacher's Magazine* editor J. B. Chapman gave Wiley a monthly vehicle to pastors by allowing him to write a theology column and feature articles. Wiley's influence among Nazarene lay people also grew after he became editor of *Herald of Holiness* in 1928.

H. Orton and Alice Wiley

Systematic theology is a crucial component of theological curriculum, and the task of writing a theology that covers the whole system of doctrine is daunting. At age 42, Wiley was commissioned in 1919 to write a systematic theology for the church. He accepted the challenge, but the first volume did not appear until 21 years later, followed a few years later by the second and third volumes.

H. Orton Wiley

Until 1940, Nazarene ministerial candidates read either John Miley's *Systematic Theology* or Thomas Ralston's *Elements of Divinity*. Both writers were Methodist theologians. When Miley's text went out of print by 1932, students were given the option of reading A. M. Hill's *Fundamental Christian Theology* in lieu of Ralston, though Ralston remained the favored text. Once the first volume of Wiley's *Christian Theology* appeared in 1940, his work supplanted all other systematic theology texts on the required course of study for ministers, and his texts were required reading for the next 45 years.

Hills and Wiley served together at Pasadena College for many years, but did not always see eye-to-eye theologically. Hills was a Holiness theologian to be sure, but he served as a minister in the Congregational Church for many years before becoming a Nazarene, and his theology took a mediating position between the Oberlin and Wesleyan approaches to Holiness theology. The Oberlin Holiness theology had been defined at Oberlin College by Charles G. Finney and Asa Mahan. This is where Hills had taken his undergraduate degree.

A. M. Hills

Wiley approached the whole matter differently. He returned to the very roots of Wesleyan thought, reaching deep behind the Americanizing tendencies that had shaped Oberlin theology and were influencing an

H. Orton Wiley and family

emergent liberal wing of early 20th-century Methodism. Theologian Carl Bangs, one of Wiley's later students, wrote that Wiley was committed to "a classical Wesleyanism." According to Bangs, Wiley wanted the Nazarenes to fully affirm their Holiness heritage, but they were "not to be a sect, cut off from Christendom. Wiley poured a whole stream of history into his perception of his church . . . [which was] to be an heir of the whole catholic tradition that had come alive in the Wesleyan revival of biblical faith."

Wiley's orientation to theology was "Anglo-Methodist." This means that he was oriented to the Protestant Reformation by way of the Anglican tradition, which took into account the writings and viewpoints of Luther and Calvin, but also sought fidelity to the theology of the early Christian centuries. Moreover, Anglicanism made room for the Arminian tradition in the 17th century, which shaped Wesley's views a century later. Wiley's orientation shaped his thinking on major issues in theology, including grace, election, baptism, and holiness. For instance, John Wesley's concept of prevenient grace was an article of faith in the Church of England and the Methodist Episcopal Church, so it was also important to Wiley. The affirmation of prevenient grace allowed Wiley to affirm the priority of faith as God's true gift to believers, while rejecting Calvinistic notions of individual predestination. Wiley appreciated that Methodism's Anglican roots opened a way for theology to appropriate the Early Church Fathers and the best of the catholic tradition, yet anchor it in the Protestant priority of salvation by grace alone. *Christian Theology* demonstrated that he believed the sources of theology should be broad.

Chapman and Wiley at Camp Meeting

*Christian Theology* extended Wiley's influence across three generations of Nazarene ministers, introducing readers to the history of

theology, major theological theories, and solid Wesleyan theology. It also brought Wiley recognition as a leading American exponent of Arminian theology. In that role, he was featured alongside Carl F. H. Henry, Geoffrey Bromiley, and Roger Nicole in *Christianity Today's* 1959 "Debate Over Divine Election." He had several student protégés whose own theological agendas were shaped by his attractive personality and his theological influence, including Mildred Bangs Wynkoop, Ross Price, Paul Culbertson, and Carl Bangs. Inspired by Wiley, Bangs became America's leading authority on James Arminius' life and work.

H. Orton Wiley died in Pasadena, California, in 1961.

H. Orton Wiley in the college chapel

**David Hynd**
***Missionary Surgeon and Pastor***

Social ministry was integral to the early Nazarene witness. As General Superintendent John Goodwin put it: "Pure religion always has and always will have two sides, purity and service. To neglect service in the welfare of others is to demonstrate a lack of purity. Holiness people should be preeminent in social service."

David Hynd

The earliest social ministries focused on maternity homes, orphanages, and city rescue missions. Then, in the 1920s and 1930s, Nazarene medicine began as a ministry of the general church as hospitals were built in China, Swaziland, and India.

Harmon Schmelzenbach sought a medical witness in southern Africa near the outset of his ministry there, but finances were provided only after the death of 10-year-old Raleigh Fitkin in surgery in 1914. His parents, Abram and Susan Fitkin, memorialized their son through charitable giving: a children's wing at Yale University's hospital, the Raleigh Fitkin-Paul Morgan Memorial Hospital in Asbury, NJ, and a Nazarene hospital in Swaziland.

The initial hospital in Swaziland was small and located in a sparsely populated area. Missionaries urged a larger one near a greater population center and received the endorsement of Rev. George Sharpe, missionary superintendent for Africa. In 1925, Swaziland's government donated land on a road leading into Bremersdorp (now Manzini).

Dr. David Hynd took the lead to build and equip the hospital. Hynd was Sharpe's son-in-law, a surgeon, and an ordained minister. His thorough education had not trained him in engineering, so he learned construction

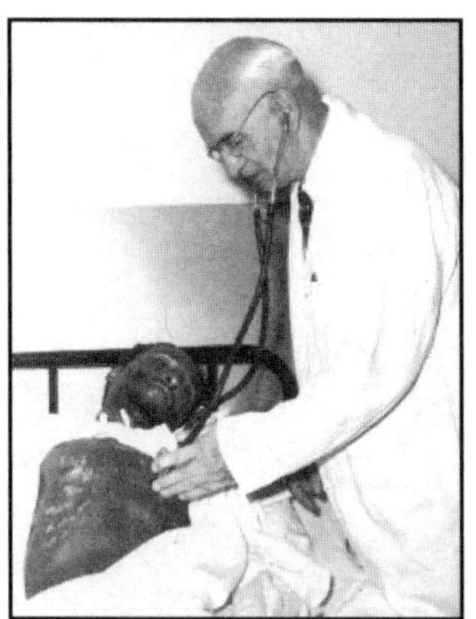
David Hynd

principles and methods from manuals, then taught them to the laborers. The hospital was completed and dedicated in 1927. As chief administrator, Hynd's steadfast hand guided the hospital until 1961.

Hynd was born in Perth, Scotland, in 1895. He earned four degrees at the University of Glasgow, including a doctorate in surgery. He took further study at the Royal College of Medicine in London. His education was interrupted for several years while he served in the armed forces during World War I. In Glasgow, he was active in the mother church of British Nazarenes, the Parkhead Church of the Nazarene founded by Sharpe in 1906. He met Agnes Kanema Sharpe, who was known as Nema. They married in 1918, and husband and wife were ordained to the ministry at the 1924 district assembly by John Goodwin. The couple were co-pastors of the Bremersdorp church and co-workers at the mission hospital. Nema had a degree in nursing, and she later received radiographer training qualifying her to take X-rays.

David Hynd receiving Commander of the British Empire honor from King George

The hospital's construction was David Hynd's first great project. Others followed. A training program for nurses began in 1928. In 1932, he founded the Red Cross of Swaziland. Over time, the hospital added new wards—for children, new mothers, surgery, and X-rays. The hospital grew to 220 beds during his tenure.

There was also a wider influence: the hospital was a hub surrounded by medical outstations and mobile clinics. For instance, Elizabeth Cole was assigned to Raleigh Fitkin Memorial Hospital as a nurse in 1935 but moved into field nursing, where she developed an interest in leprosy patients. Hynd lobbied the government on behalf of her vision, and the Mbuluzi Leper Hospital was established 40 miles from Manzini. The hospital operated it as an extension facility with Cole as the resident nurse from 1948 until her retirement.

David Hynd was active in many other affairs. For decades, he was president of the Swaziland Conference of Churches and of the Holiness Association for Africa. He was a charter member of the Swaziland Bible Society Board and a member of his adopted country's national Board of Education. His accomplishments were noted and honored. In 1947, Great Britain's King George VI toured Africa with the British royal family and

personally bestowed on Hynd the honor of Commander of the Order of the British Empire. After Swaziland's independence, he was awarded the Independence Medal (1968) and the Medal of Royal Order (1982) by King Sobhuza II. Swaziland also commemorated his life and work on postage stamps.

The arc of David and Nema Hynd's lives spanned the end of British colonial rule and the emergence of Swaziland's independence. Their love for the people was great, and they remained in Swaziland after they retired. They lived for a few years at the leprosy clinic, then moved to the capital of Mbabane. Nema Hynd died in 1982. David Hynd died in 1990 at age 95. Their funeral services were conducted in the Sharpe Memorial Church in Manzini.

Nema Hynd

**How Shall We Overcome?**
***American Blacks and the Church of the Nazarene***

The late 19th-century rise of American Holiness denominations coincided with the onset of the Jim Crow laws that institutionalized racial segregation in the states of the American South. State by state and law by law, the social relations between blacks and whites were increasingly

Gulf Central District Assembly in Chattanooga, Tennessee.
Presiding General Superintendent D. I. Vanderpool in the upper right.

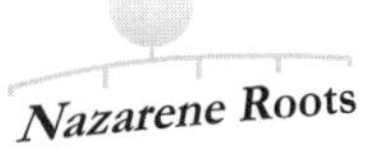



regulated by legislative and judicial action in the areas of public education and accommodations. The situation was better in the North, where segregation was not upheld by law, but where *de facto* segregation generally prevailed nonetheless.

The Holiness Movement spoke no prophetic words to this situation, and the birth of the Church of the Nazarene and other predominantly white Holiness denominations ran parallel with the rise of black ones, such as the Church of Christ (Holiness). Even the Church of God (Anderson, Indiana), which developed a sizable African-American membership rising to nearly a third of the total, developed two annual meetings in two locations, one attended by black members of the denomination, the other attended largely by its white members.

Warren Rogers

An African-American presence in the early Church of the Nazarene was real but modest. Black Nazarenes appear in early pictures of New England District deaconesses, church groups, and camp meeting participants. Rev. Mary Palmer, a black woman, was the founding pastor of the racially mixed Grace Church of the Nazarene on the Southern California District from 1909 to 1916. There were also black influences from outside the denomination. Songwriter Charles Price Jones, founder of the Church of Christ (Holiness), was a friend of J.O. McClurkan, Nazarene founder in the Southeast. Jones wrote many songs with Holiness themes that became Nazarene favorites, including “Deeper, Deeper” and “I Would Not Be Denied.”

The Church of the Nazarene’s general and district leaders were aware from an early date that the church’s efforts to reach American blacks were deplorable. Litanies confessing failure toward black Americans appeared frequently in the *Herald of Holiness* and the quadrennial addresses of the general superintendents. Writers and speakers noted that there was more grass-roots support for sending cross-cultural missionaries to Africa than for supporting black home missions in America.

R. W. Cunningham

The church nurtured relations with the Church of Christ (Holiness) until the 1940s. The denominations exchanged fraternal delegates to each other’s general meetings, and in 1922, Bishop Jones was the evangelist at the Southern California District Assembly. After A.T. Rucker from the CCH addressed the 1923 General Assembly, a special committee was ordered to pursue merger between the churches. A similar thing happened after Bishop Butler addressed the 1940 General Assembly. Nothing materialized in either instance, but individual CCH ministers transferred to the Church of the Nazarene over the years, including D.A. Murray and Boyd Proctor.

Warren Rogers

Murray pioneered a strong Nazarene work in New Orleans, while Proctor did the same in Richmond, Virginia.

Ministries to African-Americans were boosted in the 1940s and 1950s by the creation of a theological school and the Gulf Central District. E. E. Hale organized Nazarene Training College at Institute, WV, in 1948 and was president until 1954, when he was succeeded by R.W. Cunningham. Many pastors were trained there until 1970, when the school was forced to merge with Nazarene Bible College in Colorado Springs.

The Gulf Central District was, in Roger Bowman's words, "not organized as an instrument of segregation but as an instrument of evangelism." It developed out of a series of annual conferences for black churchmen that began in 1947. The district was organized in 1953 with Leon Chambers as superintendent. Warren Rogers succeeded him in 1958 and led the district until its final assembly in 1969. Nazarene Training College and the Gulf Central District both provided greater opportunity for black leadership to develop within the Church of the Nazarene.

Maynard James

## Maynard James
### *Witness of a Soul Aflame*

"Evangelism was the passion of his life, and *The Flame* was essentially its light and its reflection. Through an anointed pen as also by the Celtic fervency of advocative preaching, he pressed the urgency of scriptural Holiness as the necessary preparation for the Lord's return—His *near* return, as it always was for him—and held aloft in the promise of that climactic event the bright shining light of Israel's hope and the only answer to the world's distress and depravity. In his evangelistic ministry, he raised up, under God, more than thirty churches and helped in the founding of many others. *The Flame* was the handmaid of his ministry as well as the voice of the churches under his influence." These were the observations of Peter Gentry, a Nazarene minister in Britain, on the death of Maynard Gordon James. James was an ordained elder on the British Isles South District at the time of his death.

Maynard James was born in the mining community of Bargoed, Wales, in 1902 and died at Birkenhead, England, on May 21, 1988.

Maynard James opening Dewsbury Church of the Nazarene

Converted as a boy, James was restored and sanctified at age 17. His piety was subsequently nurtured in the local congregation of the Holiness Mission, a body formed in London in 1907 by businessman David Thomas. James emerged as a young leader of the local church and entered Cliff College in 1927, where he studied under the sainted Samuel Chadwick. Cliff College had established itself as a center for the promotion of Wesleyan-Holiness life and doctrine among Britain's Wesleyan Methodists. One other tradition was dominant at Cliff: a commitment to evangelism. Maynard James came under the spell of these two ideas—holiness and evangelism—particularly as they were joined together by Cliff's Methodist Friars. As itinerant evangelists, the Methodist Friars trekked from place to place carrying personal and evangelistic necessities on two-wheel carts.

Maynard James

James imported the concept into the International Holiness Mission. Starting in 1928, he spearheaded development of the Holiness Mission Trekkers. Over the next half-dozen years, they held a series of evangelistic campaigns that resulted in new congregations, a fresh crop of ministers, and the revitalization of the IHM. Out of the trekking movement emerged Jack Ford, Leonard Ravenhill, and Clifford Filer—strong leaders in Britain's $20^{th}$ century Holiness revival. James continued to promote trekking among other modes of evangelism. And he served as pastor of IHM congregations.

IHM founder David Thomas died in 1930. By 1934, a rift developed that separated the church's executive council lay leaders from several key pastors, including James, Ford, and Ravenhill. The pastors, all active in revival and healing campaigns, were willing to tolerate a wider range of spiritual expression than was the council. They subsequently withdrew, establishing the Calvary Holiness Church later that year to conserve their converts. James began publishing *The Flame* in 1935 and the following year it became the Calvary Holiness Church's official paper. By 1941, it had reached a circulation of 25,000 copies.

Other milestones followed. In 1937, Clifford Filer headed a group of missionaries that opened work in Colombia. A second field later opened in Pakistan. Another key event was the founding of Beech Lawn Bible College at Uppermill in 1948. It later moved to Stalybridge, near Manchester.

The spirit of reconciliation between the Calvary Holiness Church and the International Holiness Mission was effected by 1946, but talk of merger did not bear fruit for another decade, when it was finally consummated under the banner of the Church of the Nazarene, with which the IHM united

in 1952. Three years later, on June 11, 1955, the Calvary Holiness Church under the leadership of Maynard James and Jack Ford united as well, bringing 22 congregations and almost 600 members in England and Wales.

At this point, James made *The Flame* an independent paper open toward all who were committed to the Wesleyan-Holiness view of sanctification. Essentially it was a journal of "the higher Christian life." Not only Nazarenes, but Wesleyan Methodist and Pentecostal Holiness leaders paid tribute to Maynard James upon his death—reflections of the ecumenical nature of his evangelical spirit.

### H. T. Reza:
### *The Gospel of Grace in the Spanish Tongue*

H. T. Reza

Like the dinosaur tracks that hikers discovered in hard rock near a south Texas riverbed, H. T. Reza's footprints on the Nazarene canvas are large, striking in appearance, and impossible to ignore. His varied career as a pastor, educator, and headquarters executive is linked to the rise of new technologies that he mastered, then used to facilitate the Church of the Nazarene's growth throughout Latin America.

Honorato Reza was born in Alahuixtlan, in Mexico's State of Guerrero, on October 27, 1912. His schooling began at six in the home of a Protestant pastor and continued at a Nazarene boarding school in Teloloapan and later in Mexico City. He worked in exchange for his education from the time he entered grade school—a pattern of striving that reflected the enterprising spirit of the boy and later the man.

H. T. Reza

Reza was converted to Christ at eleven, after a sermon preached by Ruth Delgado. He wandered from the faith in his teens, but was reclaimed in 1930. He graduated from the church's Bible training school in Mexico City in 1935, and took his first pastorate at Matias Romero.

General Superintendent John Goodwin arranged for Reza to enter Pasadena College in 1937. He received his bachelor's degree in 1939 and returned to Mexico City to plant a new church. Goodwin ordained him that summer, and a few months later, Honorato Reza was united in marriage to Ernestina Tentori.

He continued to study while pastoring. He received an advanced degree from the University of Mexico in 1941. H. Orton Wiley invited him to Pasadena College the following year to teach Spanish language and literature. In addition to his duties in Pasadena, Reza was dean and teacher

H. T. Reza

in a Bible college in Los Angeles for the church's Spanish-speaking pastors in Southern California.

The 1944 General Assembly took two actions that altered Reza's life. It created a Spanish Department and a Nazarene Radio League. Reza, appointed to head the new Spanish Department, moved his family to Kansas City in 1946. Soon, he was involved in the church's radio ministry as well.

The post-World War era was a dynamic period for the Church of the Nazarene. Its evangelistic impulses had been restricted for several years by financial restraints and World War, but peace and newfound prosperity began putting wings under the church's dreams. Reza arrived in Kansas City at a time of heady optimism and an intense desire to achieve evangelistic goals. The Mid-Century Crusade for Souls was on.

H. T. Reza led the Spanish Department throughout its 30-year history as it developed an array of publications: curriculum, magazines, hymnals, and theological texts. *El Heraldo de Santidad* was one of these, a monthly that Reza proposed early in his tenure. This publication, like others, used some material adapted and translated from English, while other material was created for it by Spanish writers.

H. T. Reza

The department grew. It became the Latin Department when Portuguese publications were added in 1971, then the International Publications Board in 1976 with the addition of French publications and a broad mandate to supervise the publication of all non-English language materials. Reza headed IPB until 1981, a year in which it published over one million pieces of literature.

The use of radio as a tool for ministry was a growing phenomenon in the 1940s. The Nazarene Radio League originally envisioned an English-language broadcast, "Showers of Blessing," but the need to produce a Spanish broadcast was recognized eventually. Reza was tapped to be its preacher and integrated this responsibility into his ever-expanding portfolio. For 23 years, his fertile mind and deep voice preached inspiration and hope to listeners of "La Hora Nazarena" radio broadcast. At one point, "La Hora Nazarena" aired on over 700 radio stations. Reza became one of the church's most recognizable personalities.

He traveled widely in these years, and oversaw many other projects: planting a Spanish church in Kansas City, KS; hosting a Hispanic affairs program broadcast by a Kansas City TV station; and serving as liaison to Cuban Nazarenes. In the early 1980s, he became founding president of Seminario Nazareno Mexicano in Mexico City, guiding it through its early development.

H. T. Reza's ministry of the written and preached word played a crucial role in the church's growth in Latin America in the past half-century and inspired a generation of leaders who follow in his footsteps.

**Timothy L. Smith**
***The Recovery of the Nazarene Vision***

No one tracked the footprints across the Nazarene landscape better than Timothy L. Smith. Historian, pastor, teacher, and preacher, Smith embodied one of John Wesley's noblest ideals—the union of "knowledge and vital piety."

Timothy L. Smith

Smith was the product of a Nazarene home—both parents, in fact, were ministers. He was conducting revivals well before he graduated with honors in history from the University of Virginia, displaying an early commitment both to church and to learning.

He earned advanced degrees in American history at Harvard University, inheriting the interests of his mentor, Arthur Schlesinger, Sr., in urban America, social ferment, and reform. Smith's first book, *Revivalism and Social Reform*, was a major publication and has been in print since 1957. In it, Smith countered then-prevalent ideas about revivalism.

At the time, many scholars assumed that revivalism was a conservative force that impeded change, but Smith demonstrated that revivalism often expanded visions and created energies that initiated, rather than hindered, social reform. He underscored the role of evangelical abolitionists like Charles Finney and Orange Scott in the antislavery campaign, and men and women with hearts for the poor like Phoebe Palmer and B. T. Roberts, who refused to forsake the city but saw it, instead, as their venue for service. Moreover, Smith was the first to draw attention to Palmer's leadership of the early Wesleyan-Holiness movement.

*Revivalism and Social Reform* established Smith's reputation as a scholar and catapulted him into the ranks of evangelical leadership. While scholars debated its theses, evangelicals used it as a resource for

Timothy L. Smith

rediscovering their heritage. Smith's book, coupled with Carl F. H. Henry's *The Uneasy Conscience of Modern Fundamentalism* and David Moberg's *The Great Reversal,* helped evangelicals rediscover social ministry in Christ's name—a dimension of ministry largely abandoned during evangelicalism's fundamentalist phase.

Smith continued probing. He wrote pioneering essays on religion and higher education and the role of ethnicity in shaping American religion. He climbed slowly to the highest rungs of his profession, teaching American history at Johns Hopkins University and serving as president of the American Society of Church History.

So what did he regard as his most outstanding professional achievement? In 1981 or so, he responded directly to this question, citing his second book, *Called Unto Holiness* (1962), a history of Nazarene origins and early development.

*Called Unto Holiness* was a remarkable achievement in many ways. The basic materials for understanding the church's origins were scant and fugitive. Smith faced the challenge not only of writing the history, but of discovering enough original sources to actually support the project. Many of the diaries, record books, and letters that he found in private hands were eventually donated to the church archives.

Timothy L. Smith

Moreover, Smith developed a clear and cogent thesis about Nazarene origins and development that held his book together. He argued that the Church of the Nazarene cannot be understood unless we first realize that there always has been more than one Holiness tradition at work in our midst. Specifically, he saw two Holiness traditions at work among early Nazarenes—one rural and one urban. Smith contended that the marriage of these two goes far toward understanding how the church originated and why some of the tensions that characterize its life are there. That book—so richly populated with people named Bresee, Reynolds, Jernigan, Cagle, Chapman, Fitkin, Williams, Hoople, and many others—is basic reading for anyone who wants to understand this church.

Timothy Smith's fruitful life ended in 1997, but his influence lives on. He is worth remembering by everyone who wants to track the footprints across the Nazarene landscape.

CHAPTER 5

# Women Called

## Introduction

Every pastor and layperson should know two things about the ministry of women in the Church of the Nazarene. First, the Nazarene *Manual* has never barred anyone from a lay or clergy office in the church, including the ordained ministry, on the basis of gender. Second, the church's historic position is thoroughly biblical. The founders were Bible-based people, and one of their defining characteristics was the deeply-held conviction that women were included in the apostolic ministry of the New Testament church. They were convinced, as Bresee put it, that as long as the Church of the Nazarene has an apostolic ministry, then women will be a part of it.

The Church of the Nazarene originated at a time when there was a growing body of literature affirming the role of women in the ministry. Much of that literature originated within the Wesleyan-Holiness movement itself, including writings by Salvation Army co-founder Catherine Booth, Methodist laywoman Phoebe Palmer, Free Methodist general superintendents B. T. Roberts and Walter Sellew, Wesleyan Methodist Church co-founder Luther Lee, and Nazarene Fannie McDowell Hunter. All three of the founding parent bodies that merged in 1907 and 1908 affirmed that there was a biblical basis for ordaining women, and all three had acted on that conviction by ordaining tested and proven women to the ministry.

Phineas Bresee was well-acquainted with the basic thrust of this literature. During one of his last Methodist pastorates, he brought Amanda Berry Smith, a black evangelist, to preach in his Los Angeles church. After Los Angeles First Church of the Nazarene was organized, Bresee generally opened his pulpit to guest preachers on Sunday nights, and in this capacity, his list of guest preachers included women. He entrusted Phoebe Epperson with the primary preaching responsibility of Los Angeles First Church during a period when he was travelling in other states, and Lucy Knott became the pastor of another early Nazarene congregation in Los Angeles.

Elsie Wallace was the first woman ordained by Bresee. This occurred in Spokane, Washington, in 1902. Yet, women were ordained even earlier in other branches of the united church: in the South in 1899 and in the East in 1892. And women were ordained in the Pentecostal Church of Scotland three years before that denomination merged with the Pentecostal Nazarenes.

This common commitment to the full equality of women in the ministry and in the church was one of the elements that helped knit these merging denominations together. They shared a common doctrine of the ministry. This set them apart from other denominations, but it was part of the attraction to one another, and it was part of the glue that helped knit the new denomination together. The commitment to the ministry of women is a part of the Nazarene DNA.

### "Your Daughters Shall Prophesy"
### *Nazarene Women and Apostolic Ministry*

Anna Hanscome's resolve to establish a stable Holiness work in Malden, MA, led to the founding in 1890 of one of the Church of the Nazarene's ten oldest congregations. The Central Evangelical Holiness Association (our New England root) ordained her in 1892. She pastored at Malden until her death. Hanscome was one of the first women ordained in America and the first by any Nazarene parent body. The CEHA merged

with the Association of Pentecostal Churches of America in 1896, and Susan Fitkin, Martha Curry, and other preaching women soon united with it. Curry was ordained in 1902.

In the South, Susie Sherman and Emma Woodcock preached daily for two months beside Robert Lee Harris in a Tennessee revival that launched the New Testament Church of Christ in 1894. Mary Lee Cagle and Elliott J. Sheeks were ordained by its Eastern Council in 1899. Cagle had already organized a circle of churches near Abilene, TX, that formed the nucleus of today's West Texas District. In east Texas, Independent Holiness Church preacher Johnny Hill Jernigan was ordained in 1902 in the same service as C. B. Jernigan, her husband. The merger of these southern groups in 1904 was followed by the publication of a remarkable book edited by Fannie McDowell Hunter, pastor in Rising Star, TX. *Women Preachers* featured nine women's "call narratives" and marshaled arguments defending women's public ministry. By 1908, one sixth of the Holiness Church of Christ's 178 ordained ministers were women.

Mattie Wines,
Indianapolis District

On the west coast, Phineas Bresee employed Amanda Berry Smith, a noted black preacher, as the evangelist in 1890 at Los Angeles' Asbury Methodist Church. In 1895, under his guidance, Los Angeles First Church of the Nazarene provided for women to preach at the time of its founding. In 1902, Bresee ordained Elsie Wallace, founding pastor of Spokane, WA, First Church. He ordained Lucy Knott, founding pastor of a second Los Angeles congregation, the next year.

Most denominations of that day severely restricted women's participation in church governance and ministry, even locally. However, early Nazarenes opened every clergy and lay office to female initiative, whether at the local, district, or general level.

Lura Horton,
New England District

The *concept of an apostolic ministry*—a simple but explosive idea, long since ignored—lay behind this openness to women's voices and gifts. The basic idea of *apostolicity* is that something conforms to or reflects the belief and practice of the New Testament church.

The Wesleyan tradition's linkage of *women* and *apostolic ministry* stemmed from various sources, including John Wesley's conviction that the church is essentially "the people of God," not a clergy hierarchy, and that every Christian bears the gospel and is a minister in his or her own

Emma Irick,
Dallas District

Agnes Diffee,
Arkansas District

way. Thus, Grace Murray and Mary Bosanquet were among the lay people whom Wesley permitted to preach.

The 19th century Wesleyan-Holiness movement developed the idea further. Phoebe Palmer's *Promise of the Father* (1859) grounded women's right to preach in Peter's sermon on Pentecost and his resounding declaration: "This is that spoken of by the prophet Joel: 'In the last days,' says the Lord, 'I will pour out my spirit on all flesh . . . and your sons and daughters shall prophesy.'" Thus, the very gift of God's Spirit to the Christian church establishes and empowers a gender-inclusive ministry, and one does not deny women their apostolic right to preach without denying the Spirit who calls the Church into being. Other writers emphasized different scriptural texts. Wesleyan Methodist leader Luther Lee emphasized Gal. 3:28 as the basis for women's ministry, as did Catherine Booth, Salvation Army co-founder, in *Female Ministry; or, Woman's Right to Preach the Gospel*. The Nazarene founders, steeped in this growing body of exegetical literature, defended the practice of ordaining women by drawing freely on Peter and Paul alike.

Thus, Bresee's declaration to the Second General Assembly's manual revision committee had specific content behind it. Asserting that the Church of the Nazarene had *an apostolic ministry*, he argued that women's right to preach and pursue ordination was sufficiently safeguarded *so long as apostolicity was the hallmark* of the church's ministry. C. E. Brown, leader in another Holiness denomination, later summarized the conviction this way: "The prevalence of women preachers is a fair measure of the spirituality of a church, a country, or an age. As the church grows more apostolic and more deeply spiritual, women preachers and workers abound in that church; as it grows more worldly and cold, the ministry of women is despised and gradually ceases altogether." The inclusion of women was not simply an "add-on" to traditional notions of Christian ministry, but represented altogether a radically different doctrine of the ministry held by the more progressive Holiness churches.

This intention to open wide the doors to women's leadership was celebrated publicly from the first. Lura Horton and Anna Cooley were among the seven new ministers ordained at the First General Assembly in Chicago (1907). The next year, at Pilot Point, TX, Mary Emily Ellyson was ordained beside R. T. Williams and Alpin Bowes at the Second General

Assembly. Women subsequently assumed a wide variety of ministerial roles in Nazarene life.

Eight women on the Southern California District's 1922 clergy roll were missionaries: Myrtle Mangum and Lou Jane Hatch in India; Minnie Staples in Japan; Mrs. Harry Wiese in China; Pearl Ingram in Central America; and Etta Innis Shirley, Maud Cretors, and Louise Robinson in Africa. Esther Carson Winans was an ordained minister who relied on her pastoral experience during missionary service in Peru. The Scottish missionary to Swaziland, Agnes Kanema Hynd, was not only a medical professional, but an ordained minister like her mother, Jane Sharpe of Glasgow.

Santos Elizondo, Southwest Spanish District

Women shaped home missions. Maye McReynolds led the Church of the Nazarene into ministry to Hispanics. One of her converts in Los Angeles, Santos Elizondo, pioneered home mission churches in Texas and Mexico alike. Minnie Staples' ministry among Japanese immigrants in Southern California preceded her missionary service in Japan, while Lillian Poole returned from Japan to start a Japanese-American ministry on the San Francisco District. Mary Lee Cagle planted Lubbock, TX, First Church and at least 21 other congregations in six states.

"And the thought of me, a Mexican woman, starting a church—impossible—but when I looked to the Lord I saw all things were possible to them that love the Lord."
—Rev. Santos Elizondo

Scores of women have been Nazarene evangelists. Minnie Ludwig conducted revivals with her husband, Theodore. Joy and Mary Latham were full-time evangelists before joining the Nazarene Headquarters staff. Juliet Ndzimandze conducted revivals throughout Swaziland before her ministry took her across a wide swath of Africa. Dell Aycock, Nettie Miller, Elizabeth Vennum, and Nettie Hudson are among the revivalists whose voices once resounded from Nazarene pulpits.

And there were pastors. Agnes Diffee, Little Rock First Church's senior pastor for 18 years, was renowned throughout Arkansas and led one of the denomination's largest congregations. Emma Irick's church in Lufkin, TX, was the largest in the Houston District. Rosa Lee served nearly a decade as pastor of her district's largest church when she became superintendent of the Leeward/Virgin Islands District. Bessie Dillingham, grandmother of Focus on the Family executives James Dobson and H. B. London, Jr., co-pastored 10 churches, including Shreveport (LA) and Oklahoma City First Churches, with husband, M. V. Dillingham. Like many clergy couples, they divided the preaching responsibilities, and "Sister Dill"

usually preached an evangelistic sermon at the Sunday evening service. Lucy Knott, Martha Curry, Elsie Wallace, and many others devoted their lives largely to pastoral ministry.

Jane Sharpe,
British Isles District

Mary Emily Ellyson taught in the religion departments of several Nazarene colleges. Maude Stuneck, whose "classes were always packed out," did so at Trevecca and contributed to the *Beacon Bible Commentary.* New Testament specialist Olive Winchester—the first woman ordained in Scotland by any denomination—taught religion at Northwest Nazarene College, where she was also academic dean and vice president, and at Pasadena College.

Mildred Bangs Wynkoop served multiple roles: evangelist, missionary (Taiwan and Japan), and theological educator. Her *Theology of Love* remains a popular study in the theology of Christian Holiness. Argentinian preacher Lucía Carmen García de Costa was one of the most effective church planters in Nazarene history. But de Costa, who had a doctorate in linguistics, also taught at the Nazarene Bible college in Buenos Aires and translated Wesleyan theological texts into Spanish.

Does the Church of the Nazarene lay claim to an apostolic ministry today in a way that Bresee and other founders would honor? Nazarene Researcher Rich Houseal studied the development of Nazarene women clergy in the U.S. and found that their ministerial opportunities increased throughout the 1920s and 1930s, but experienced a sharp decline after the mid-1950s.

Our history points back to a solution. The recovery of a biblical understanding of apostolic ministry is part of the church's theological task. Our history teaches that setting God's people free for ministry is a distinguishing hallmark of the Wesleyan vision.

**Elliott J. Sheeks**
***Pastor and Religion Professor***

Elliott J. Deboe was 18, and on the cusp of adulthood, when she heard Rev. Louisa Woosley preach in a Kentucky revival. The moment transfixed her. It was 1890, and Woosley, a Cumberland Presbyterian, was opening doors throughout the Upper South for women to preach. Elliott

Deboe took it all in, little realizing that within seven years she, too, would step behind the pulpit and assume the role of a gospel preacher.

Elliott Deboe was the second of nine children born to Kentucky farmers. She joined the Cumberland Presbyterian Church, the church of her mother, at age 11. In 1891, she married Edwin H. Sheeks, an affluent businessman some years her senior. She traveled with him for two years before they settled in Memphis, joined one of the city's more fashionable churches, and settled into a conventional domestic life. But other forces already set in motion would alter their lives.

Elliott J. Sheeks

Elliott and Edwin Sheeks were soon drawn into the orbit of another Memphis resident, Robert Lee Harris, a youthful and engaging revivalist. Harris was a classic religious dissenter. As a youth in Texas, he gravitated to the Free Methodist Church, a predominantly Yankee sect sprung from the soil of abolitionism, thus anathema to most white Southerners. Harris also became aligned with a radical wing of Free Methodism that accepted women as preachers and sought their right to ordination. Though ordained to the ministry at the hands of B. T. Roberts, the Free Methodist founder, Harris eventually hoped to widen his sphere of influence and transferred his membership to the culturally dominant Methodist Episcopal Church, South. However, he was irrevocably marked by his Free Methodist years and never fit easily into the M.E.C., South. When Elliott and Edwin Sheeks first met him, Harris was already on a collision course with southern Methodist leadership.

Elliott J. Sheeks

In the summer of 1894, Harris announced that he could no longer belong to a church with bishops and formed an independent Wesleyan-Holiness congregation in Milan, Tennessee, known as the New Testament Church of Christ. Edwin Sheeks, with some reluctance, and Elliott Sheeks, with some enthusiasm, joined the new church as charter members.

Harris was a dying man. Tuberculosis claimed his life in November. His church should have withered away, but extraordinary lay people—mainly women—assumed new roles as pastors and evangelists. His widow, Mary Lee Harris, emerged within a year as an active revivalist and a planter of new congregations. Milan businessman Balie Mitchum and his wife, Donie, became lay preachers. And Elliott Sheeks acknowledged a growing sense of divine purpose and preached her first sermon while assisting Harris in a revival in Monette, AR. A swelling network of churches led to the first

general council in 1899, at which Mary Lee Harris, Elliott J. Sheeks, and George Hammond were ordained to the ministry.

Elliott J. Sheeks

Harris' primary focus was in western Texas, where she planted churches, married cowboy Henry Cagle, and organized the denomination's Texas Council. Elliott Sheeks assisted the Mitchums in Tennessee at first, then struck out to plant churches in Arkansas, where the bulk of the Eastern Council's congregations were located by 1905. Mrs. E. A. Masterman became Elliott Sheeks' traveling companion and song evangelist as the latter itinerated from her home in Memphis to keep her pastoral appointments.

Often E. J. Sheeks was the pastor of more than one church at a time. In 1904, for instance, she was the pastor of three congregations in Tennessee—located at Hillville, Luray, and Beech Bluff—and a fourth located in Stony Point, Arkansas. In her annual report to the Eastern Council at the close of the year, Sheeks noted that she had preached 182 sermons, and "traveled 7,600 miles in gospel work." She commented: "The churches of which I am pastor are all in good spiritual condition. There are good Sunday Schools and the prayer meetings run winter and summer." She also voiced her agreement with a decision taken that year merging the New Testament Church of Christ with another southern body to form the Holiness Church of Christ.

She likewise performed yeoman service as secretary from 1899 to 1908 of the Eastern Council, taking and preserving the official minutes of the council's annual meetings, receiving and filing annual reports from each minister and congregation, maintaining the official roster of ministers, and signing ordination credentials. As secretary, she was the council's second ranking officer, and her willingness to assume the duty each year provided stability, since the council's presidency changed nearly every year.

She also served as a fraternal delegate to the First General Assembly of the Church of the Nazarene held in 1907 in Chicago. Shortly after returning from that event, her glowing report of that assembly to the Eastern Council ended in her motion, unanimously approved, to unite with the Nazarenes. That decision, and a similar one by the Texas Council, paved the way for the Holiness Church of Christ to merge with the Church of the Nazarene one year later at Pilot Point, TX, north of Dallas.

The 1908 merger resulted in much of the old Eastern Council becoming the new Arkansas District, which Elliott Sheeks continued serving as

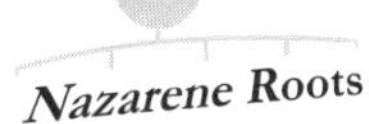


district secretary and pastor of various churches until 1915. She was a persistent advocate for establishing a home for pregnant unwed girls, which eventually opened in Texarkana as a joint project of the Arkansas and Dallas Districts. In 1915, she and her husband moved to Greenville, TX, where she earned a bachelor's degree in theology at a small Nazarene college. She continued to pastor congregations in Texas and served as Dallas District secretary from 1915 until 1923.

Elliott J. Sheeks

In 1925, she embarked on a new career: professor of religion at Bresee College in Hutchinson, KS. There, she taught Christian missions, church history, and general introductory Bible courses. She also earned a second bachelor's degree at nearby Sterling College, a Presbyterian school. She taught at Bresee College until it merged in 1939 with present-day Southern Nazarene University in Oklahoma. Edwin Sheeks died in Hutchinson in 1935. E. J. Sheeks died there 11 years later and was buried back near her hometown of Marion, KY.

**Rebecca Krikorian**
***The Errand of Mercy***

The Nazarene work in Jerusalem began in 1921 under Samuel Krikorian, an ethnic Armenian who was a native of Turkey. Keen, highly motivated, and an experienced organizer, he began his ministry among those from his homeland who had been displaced by massacres and war. In 1924, he married Hranous Yardumian, an Armenian émigré from Yozgat, Turkey, who had fled as a youth to Lebanon. Their ministry in Jerusalem later extended into other parts of Jordan and into Lebanon, continuing until 1958.

Rebecca Krikorian

Another story lies behind Samuel's. It is the story of his aunt Rebecca. She was the 8th of 13 children of Rev. Krikore Harootunian, a convert of missionaries sent to Turkey by the American Board of Commissioners for Foreign Missions. Rebecca became an active Christian worker while still a child. By her mid-teens, she was a Bible woman instructing children and adult females. In her late-teens, she led 70 Christian women whose outreach extended to over 900 people; conducted a school for poor children; was YWCA president; taught a women's Sunday School class with

100 members; supervised another class that encompassed 400 children; and was organizer and leader of a women's group called "Followers of Holiness." She went to London for nurses' training in obstetrics and returned to Turkey in 1892, where she was the attending midwife when her nephew Samuel was born the following year.

Rebecca Krikorian with Frances Willard

Soon, she combined gospel and obstetric work with temperance reform. In 1895, she went to London as a delegate to the World Convention of the Women's Christian Temperance Union. There, she met Frances Willard, the celebrated American temperance reformer, who urged her to go on to America to solicit funds for her work among alcoholics and addicts in Turkey. Rebecca did so and was in New York City when news arrived of the massacres carried out against the Armenian population of her native land.

Rebecca Krikorian became an activist on behalf of Armenian refugees who were scattering across Europe and eventually to America, as well as along the eastern Mediterranean. Much of her own family joined this diaspora, some coming to America, while other brothers moved their families to Syria. Her father and a brother, the latter a Yale-educated minister, continued to lead congregations in Turkish Armenia. When not active in relief work, Rebecca participated in gospel work with the Christian and Missionary Alliance and the Brethren in Christ Church.

Samuel Krikorian in Jerusalem with H. F. Reynolds

Samuel came to America for school in 1911, and Rebecca arranged for him to attend Messiah Bible School in Grantham, PA. While travelling the following year on behalf of Armenian relief, Rebecca came into contact with the Church of the Nazarene at Newton, KS, where pastor Fred Mendell helped shape an itinerary that took her to Nazarene churches throughout the West. In Los Angeles, she met Phineas Bresee, spoke in Los Angeles and Pasadena First churches and at Pasadena College. She joined the Nazarenes and settled in Pasadena.

Through his aunt's influence, Samuel Krikorian entered Pasadena College in 1914. He completed his bachelor's degree in three years, then devoted over a year as a lecturer and organizer for the Intermountain Branch of the American Committee for Armenian and Syrian Relief. Meanwhile, he and Rebecca developed a plan for a mission in Jerusalem—a plan accepted enthusiastically by the Board of Foreign Missions of the Church of the Nazarene.

Thus, a chapter began in Nazarene history that was rooted in the social solidarity of a persecuted people and the compassionate ministry of a remarkable woman on an errand of mercy.

**Olive Winchester**
***A Life in Theology and Higher Education***

Eugene Emerson's imagination was captured by a visit to Nazarene University in Pasadena in 1912. The taciturn Emerson, founder of an Idaho lumber company, had recently professed entire sanctification and cast his lot with the Wesleyan-Holiness people. After meeting with Phineas Bresee and H. Orton Wiley on his visit to California, Emerson returned to Nampa and organized support for a new school that opened the following year. Wiley came to be its president in 1917 and devoted the next decade to improving the institution—Northwest Nazarene College—financially and academically.

Olive M. Winchester

Wiley's vital task was to recruit qualified faculty who blended spiritual graces with keenly honed intellect. And none met his expectations better than Olive Winchester (1880-1947), one of the best-educated Nazarenes of her day, who followed him to Nampa later that year.

In 1902, Winchester earned her bachelor's degree from Radcliffe, the women's college associated with Harvard University. Her Harvard instructor in Semitic languages regarded her as "a student of exceptional ability." After Radcliffe, she broke new ground at the University of Glasgow as the first woman admitted to and graduated from the Bachelor of Divinity program.

She also opened up another door while studying in Scotland. She attended the Parkhead Pentecostal Church, the "mother church" of the Pentecostal Church of Scotland. Her application for ordination to the ministry forced the young denomination to clarify its stand on the issue. Rev. George Sharpe, the denomination's founder, supported her case. The decision was made to permit women's ordination, and, in 1912, Winchester became the first woman of any denomination to be ordained in Scotland. Among the happy outcomes of this decision were these two: Jane Sharpe, George's wife, had emerged as a lay preacher and was ordained a few years later, while their daughter, Kanema Hynd, was ordained alongside her husband, David, before the couple set out for Swaziland as medical missionaries, where they wrote their own chapter in Nazarene missions history. Winchester's involvement in the Pentecostal Church of Scotland helped it clarify its doctrine of the ministry, and as a bridge between that denomination and the Pentecostal Church of the Nazarene, she played a role in facilitating their merger in 1915.

Olive M. Winchester

Winchester returned to America to teach religion at Eastern Nazarene College. Then she moved to Berkeley, California, to earn the S. T. M. degree (Master of Sacred Theology) from the Pacific School of Religion. She met Wiley there and soon received his invitation to join the faculty at Nampa.

Throughout her tenure at Northwest Nazarene, Winchester taught her specialties: Biblical language and literature. But she also grew interested in the whole idea of religious education in the local church; and at Northwest Nazarene, she developed and taught the initial courses in religious education. She spurred further interest in that emerging discipline by contributing frequent articles on religious education to church papers and curriculum resource manuals.

President Wiley appreciated good talent—and Olive. She was elected vice-president of the college in 1922 and appointed academic dean the following year, filling both administrative roles simultaneously (and teaching) until 1935, when she resigned. A history of the college's first quarter-century summarized her contribution: "She contributed very much to the development of the right attitude toward scholastic standards, and as vice-president and dean of the college, had much to do with the internal organization of the institution." Her early labors were not in vain; others built upon them, and a half-century later, Northwest Nazarene had emerged as one of the outstanding Christian liberal arts colleges of the northwestern United States.

Despite her busy years in Nampa, Winchester's professional development progressed. She earned the Th.D. (Doctor of Theology) degree from Drew University in 1925.

Her differences with President Russell V. DeLong precipitated her resignation in 1935. Wiley again came through, inviting her to teach theology at Pasadena College, where he had returned in 1927. She taught there until her death 12 years later.

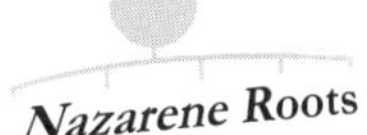


Winchester had earned high marks in biblical criticism at Glasgow, but was conservative in her application of this knowledge within the Nazarene context. Her books included studies of Moses, the prophets, and the life of Jesus. Her *Crisis Experiences in the Greek New Testament* (1953) stood in the linguistic-exegetical tradition pioneered by Daniel Steele, a Methodist scholar at Boston University. Steele defended the doctrine of entire sanctification by a study of the Greek aorist tense, and Winchester appropriated his agenda and attempted to develop it further, though this approach has since fallen out of favor with many Wesleyan-Holiness biblical scholars.

She also wrote for a variety of church periodicals, including *The Young People's Journal* for Nazarene high school youth, where, for many years, she had a standing column. In it, she explored topics ranging from Christian history to the relationship between theology and science. The religion and science series ran throughout 1931, and in it, she expressed her opposition to biological evolution, but stated her grounds for belief in cosmic and geological evolution.

She rejected the premillennialist perspective that, over her lifetime, grew in popularity within the church. Reflecting the New England tradition of Wesleyan-Holiness biblical scholarship shaped by Daniel Steele, she was an amillennialist and interpreted the Book of Revelation as a coded record of events that had occurred in the New Testament era, perhaps during Nero's reign, not predictions of the future.

Winchester was not the only woman to teach religion at Nazarene colleges during her lifetime. For much briefer spans, so did Emily Ellyson, Myrtle Mangum White, and Elliott J. Sheeks. But Winchester far surpassed them in academic background and achievement, paving the way for other professional female theologians in the church, including Maude Stuneck at Trevecca; the incomparable Mildred Wynkoop, who encountered Winchester as a freshman at Northwest Nazarene College; Diane Leclerc at Northwest Nazarene University; and Jeanne Serrao at Mount Vernon Nazarene University.

**Lucía de Costa**
***Uniting Knowledge and Vital Piety***

Lucía Carmen García was born into a middle-class family in Buenos Aires in 1903. As a child, she had high educational aspirations, envisioning herself as a future university graduate. Her exemplary piety led her to participate in many church groups, including the Daughters of Mary. She felt called, especially, to bring the Catholic faith to Argentina's rural Indians and applied to a Franciscan school for training. She was advised to complete school and reapply.

Lucía Carmen G. de Costa

A misfortune forced the Garcías from their nice home into a boarding house, where the C. H. Miller family, newly arrived missionaries, also came to live. Lucía attended devotions in the Millers's apartment and experienced an evangelical conversion in 1919. She was the first Nazarene convert in Argentina. She testified to the grace of entire sanctification the following year.

She became a full-time Christian worker. She and two other women were in the first class of seven Argentinians who received preachers licenses in 1924. She was the first graduate of the Nazarene training school for Christian workers in 1927 and became a licensed district minister the following year. She was in Argentina's first class of ordinands when J. B. Chapman conducted the district assembly in 1931.

Natalio and Lucía Carmen G. de Costa in Mendoza, Argentina

Her public ministry was diverse: pastor, church planter, evangelist, and educator. In the early and mid-1920s, she evangelized and led Bible studies at various sites in greater Buenos Aires with Soledad Quintana. In 1927, she became pastor of a circuit of churches that included Merlo, Morón, and Moreno. Three years later, her circuit included two additional churches at Castelar and Ituzaingó. The first Nazarene church building in Argentina was erected at Castelar under her leadership.

In 1935, Lucía married Natalio Costa, an Italian immigrant who had united with the church in Castelar. Her lifelong thirst for knowledge had not abated, and she refocused her ministry at this time, teaching until 1953 at the Nazarene Bible Institute in Buenos Aires. She continued to pastor churches on the weekends and entered the University of Buenos Aires. She mastered nine languages, including Hebrew, Greek, and Latin, and was awarded a doctorate in linguistics in 1950. Lucía used her linguistic skills in editorial and translation work.

Lucía and Natalio de Costa

Among her early translations were Hannah Whitall Smith's devotional classic *The Christian's Secret of a Happy Life,* J. O. McClurkan's *Wholly Sanctified,* and Amos Binney's *Theological Compend.* Later, she translated half of the abridged version of Adam Clarke's commentary and several volumes of the *Beacon Bible Commentary.* She also edited the holiness paper, *La Via Mas Excelente.*

In 1953, her ministry changed course. She and Natalio turned to church planting, organizing and nurturing seven churches over the next 16 years. Lucía did most of the preaching and pastoral care, while Natalio distributed Bibles and other Christian literature and engaged in extensive witnessing. They returned to Buenos Aires in 1969, and Lucía resumed teaching in the Bible Institute. Even so, the Costas planted one more church—that in San Antonio de Padua. In 1972, retiring missionary John Cochran praised the Costas for organizing one third of the district's 39 churches.

Lucía remained active until her 80th year and died in 1984. Natalio preceded her in death the year before.

Johnny H. Jernigan in Bethany

## Johnny Hill Jernigan
### *Mother, Revivalist and Social Worker*

Do the calls of God ever conflict with one another? When a married woman is called into Christian ministry, does it conflict with her call to be a wife and mother? Nazarene women evangelists and pastors in the southwestern United States faced this question a century ago. Johnny Hill Jernigan was one of these.

Johnny Jernigan was from northeast Texas' hill country, where Southern culture intersected the conditions and spirit of the West. The South in the late 19th century assigned each person a distinct social role

Young Jernigan Family

based on external factors: blacks were to be subordinate to whites, women were to be subordinate to men, and woe to all those who "rocked the boat." The West bred more self-reliant spirits and tended to undermine rigid thinking about assigned social class. Jernigan, the product of this environment, was a typical Southern woman until an experience of divine grace altered her sense of *who* and *what* she should be.

She first testified to the grace of entire sanctification in 1895, while she and her husband lived in Greenville, TX. Her desire to share the Good News was immediate and strong. She began to minister as a Methodist laywoman. A decade later, she looked back: "My work seemed to be among the poor, despised, and outcast of earth that no one else cared for. . . . While others were concerned about [those] across the ocean, I went to see the woman across the street. . . . God has given me a definite message to wives and mothers."

In Queens, NY

Her husband, C. B. Jernigan, also testified to entire sanctification at about this time and began preaching. Soon the Jernigans conducted revivals as a team. C. B. Jernigan encouraged his wife to develop her own preaching abilities, and both were ordained to the ministry by Seth C. Rees in 1902. One year later, a committee of four, including both Jernigans, laid hands on future Nazarene leader J. B. Chapman and ordained him to the ministry.

One night as she preached, the tender response of one in her audience, an unwed mother of two, launched Johnny Jernigan on a ministry of hunting "poor outcast girls" and persuading them to reform their lives. The first woman to enter the Berachah Rescue Home in Arlington, TX, was a prostitute taken there by Jernigan. Her mission led her to the brothels, saloons, and street corners of Dallas, Ft. Worth, Waco, Little Rock, and other cities of the Southwest, where she witnessed to her faith and offered prostitutes a way out. She often stood up to drunks and saloon owners. An angry brothel manager once aimed and fired her revolver at Jernigan, angry that Jernigan was convincing "girls" to leave "the business."

"Woman's work for woman" was a concept uppermost in her philosophy of pastoral care. It was intertwined with strong maternal instincts and her own self-image as a preacher and a mother of five children. She wrote:

"God has given me a mother's heart and a mother's love for poor erring girls; and it is my delight to go into haunts of shame and hunt them up and lead them back to a life of purity." Motherhood was no hindrance to her ministry but the motive power behind it!

Johnny Jernigan writing

By 1906, the Jernigans lived in Pilot Point, TX, headquarters community of the Holiness Church of Christ. Johnny Jernigan became financial agent of the Rest Cottage Home for unwed mothers and edited the "Rescue Work" page in the *Holiness Evangel,* the denominational paper. She published *Redeemed Through the Blood, or The Power of God to Save the Fallen*, a booklet on her ministry. Her writing style tended to be melodramatic, and articles bore titles such as "A Tragic Night in the Slums." She traveled extensively on behalf of the home and typically conducted the "rescue night" service at revivals and camp meetings.

In 1908, Johnny Jernigan was hostess to Phineas and Maria Bresee during the great uniting General Assembly at Pilot Point. A few months later, the Jernigans moved to Oklahoma, where C. B. Jerngian was the newly appointed district superintendent. Joining other families, the couple helped carve a new community named Bethany in the blackjack woods west of Oklahoma City. The philosophy of social service behind early Bethany was implied in the village's three focal points: Oklahoma Holiness College (now Southern Nazarene University); the Oklahoma Orphanage, led by the Rev. Mattie Mallory; and the Nazarene Home, a ministry for pregnant unwed teens that Johnny Jernigan organized around the Rest Cottage model.

Johnny laughing with children

Johnny Jernigan proved an able administrator of the Nazarene Home. In 1909, she launched *Highways and Hedges*, "a monthly journal devoted to the rescue work and the organ of the Nazarene Home." The home operated for seven years until Jernigan retired, citing her declining health. It cared for over seven hundred women and girls during its existence.

Johnny Hill Jerngian died in Nashville, TN in 1940. A local newspaper cited her as a resident "well-known in religious and social welfare circles." She had filled the roles of slum worker, social work publicist and promoter, financial agent, editor, matron, and evangelist, demonstrating that the experience of being a wife and mother could inform Christian ministry and social service.

**Mattie Mallory**
***The Orphan's Advocate***

Mattie Mallory

Her name was Mattie Mallory, and she had a compassionate heart for orphan children. She was the founder of Nazarene social work in the Southwest, starting both the Oklahoma Orphanage and the Peniel Orphanage before 1902. J. T. Roberts assisted in her work in Oklahoma City and Pilot Point, Texas, before launching Rest Cottage, his ministry to unwed mothers.

Mattie Mallory was born in Ottawa, Kansas, in 1865. Historian Charles Edwin Jones notes that Ottawa was near "the heart of 'bleeding Kansas'" and that her parents "were apparently part of the tide of free-staters and abolitionists [flooding] into the area before and during the Civil War." Mallory graduated from Baker University, a Methodist college, and began teaching after a further year of study at the teachers' college in Emporia. In 1892, she became principal of Dawes Academy in Berwyn, Indian Territory. The school was part of an American Baptist home mission work within the Chickasaw nation. In Berwyn, she made contact with the Holiness Movement, albeit in the aberrant form of the Fire-Baptized Holiness Association (which held to three works of grace: conversion, entire sanctification, and the baptism of the Holy Spirit).

In September 1897, Mallory started an orphans' school in Oklahoma City. By January, an orphanage with 12 children was in place. Mallory sought financial backers, found them among the Fire-Baptized people, and the Oklahoma Orphanage was incorporated in 1899. She broke with the Fire-Baptized folk the next year, however, and in 1901, her work was endorsed by the Holiness Association of Texas. C. B. Jernigan later called Mallory a decisive force in establishing a "safe work" (orthodox and void of fanaticism) in the state. *The Guide*, edited by Mallory, was the orphanage's official paper. It shows that various people later associated with the Nazarene center in Pilot Point were linked to the orphanage's early ministry.

In 1901, Mallory established a branch, the Franklin Orphan's Home, at Pilot Point, Texas. It moved to Peniel in 1902, becoming an institution of the state Holiness association. Another branch orphanage, the Bethesda Home and Mission, operated for a time in Wynnewood, Indian Territory (now Oklahoma), under her direction.

Meanwhile, Mallory moved the main school and orphanage away from downtown Oklahoma City. Using her inheritance, she purchased rural property north of the city and relocated the children. Three years later, they moved farther out and founded the Beulah Heights community, where a colony of Holiness folk gathered around her enterprises, which soon included a home for unwed mothers. The Oklahoma Orphanage and Rescue Commission was created to administer the orphanage and mother's home. Mallory was also a cofounder of the Holiness Association of Oklahoma and Indian Territory.

Children of the Oklahoma Orphanage

The Beulah Heights colony was considering yet another move when C. B. Jernigan arrived in 1909 to organize the Oklahoma-Kansas District of the Pentecostal Church of the Nazarene. Mattie Mallory and her associates united with the Nazarenes at this time. The Beulah Heights property was sold to purchase land west of the city, where the community of Bethany was planted. Her social ministries became the core institutions of the new town. Her school for orphan children became the elementary department of Oklahoma Holiness College. Mallory perceived, however, that in the competition for church dollars, some of the enterprises might not survive. She refused to place the orphanage under church control and it survived, while the Nazarene Home for unwed mothers directed by Jernigan closed after seven years.

In 1912, Mallory married R. W. Morgan. She directed the orphanage until 1920, when she turned it over to civic women who founded the metropolitan Children's Welfare League. She became a chiropractor and practiced in Oklahoma City. She died in 1938. In the meantime, she had become a Methodist. The orphanage was reorganized in 1940 as the

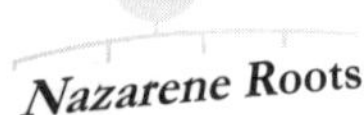


Children's Convalescent Center. It is known today simply as The Children's Center and still operates in Bethany.

The Peniel Orphanage, a spin-off of Mattie Mallory's ministry, cared for scores of children and was operated by the church's General Orphanage Board until 1929. Evangelists Oscar Hudson and Theodore Ludwig were active proponents of the orphanage until its end.

## The Two "Mrs. Chapmans"
### *Maud Frederick and Louise Robinson*

### Maud Frederick

J. B. and Maud Chapman

By Louise Chapman's death in 1993, many regarded her as *the* Mrs. J. B. Chapman. And yet the wife of Chapman's youth, the mother of his seven children, and his companion for 37 years was Maud Frederick. Two women graced his life in marriage. Both were pioneers: Maud as an early revival and home mission worker; Louise as a foreign missionary and church leader. They shared several characteristics but lived fundamentally different lives.

Maud Frederick was born on her grandfather's farm near Longview, TX, on December 3, 1880. Her mother died when Maud was six. Her father moved his family of small children to Palestine, TX, where she attended public school. At 15, she was sent to a school in Waco. She entered the state teacher's college at Huntsville at 17, finished a one-year course, then became a schoolteacher.

She shared a Baptist heritage, but was influenced by Methodist revivalists. Her conversion, at 16, was in a meeting led by the famed Methodist preacher Sam Jones. Maud was baptized and joined a Baptist church. She became a Methodist in 1899, however, after being sanctified under the ministry of Will Huff, a Methodist evangelist and close colleague of Bud Robinson. Her new pastor, John Paul, was a popular Holiness leader in the South.

She met J. B. Chapman in early 1902. A young preacher, he was holding a revival in Troup, where she was visiting. Her diary does not mention their first meeting, but that spring she joined the Chapman-

Tetrick evangelistic party for several weeks. The diary soon mentioned "Brother Jimmie." That fall and winter, she taught school at Iron Bluff and White's Chapel, resigning one month before C. B. Jernigan performed their wedding service on February 18, 1903. Her new husband preached later that very night. The next day, they took a train to Indian Territory (now Oklahoma) and started a revival.

Chapmans in front of the church in Kyoto, Japan

Their early marriage was spent in Oklahoma, briefly in Phillips, then at Durant, where they planted a church. Poverty was the lot of early Nazarene home missionaries, but Maud's photograph shows a spirited woman.

Lois was born in Durant. Other babies followed: James (who died at five months), then Grace, Harold, Brilhart, Gertrude, and Paul.

The years brought other changes. In 1904, their group, the Independent Holiness Church, became part of the Holiness Church of Christ, which united in turn with the Nazarenes in 1908. J. B. Chapman's star gradually rose: president of the HCC's General Council; then Nazarene district superintendent; president of colleges in Arkansas and Texas; pastor of Bethany First Church; editor of *Herald of Holiness*; and, in 1928, general superintendent. They relocated their home often. There was also grief: Brilhart died young, at 25.

Because of Maud Chapman's maternal duties, she and her husband were apart frequently as he spoke to churches and camps, and later presided over assemblies. She went with him when possible, but they were separated for 10 months in 1931 when he visited districts around the world. Never again, he vowed upon his return. After that, she always traveled with him overseas—to Japan, Asia, the Middle East, Europe, and the West Indies between 1933 and 1940.

J. B. and Maud Chapman with Lois, home mission pastors in Oklahoma

While J. B. Chapman enjoyed the quality of his wife's testimonies, her ministry grew wider than the local church. She spoke to groups about Nazarene missions after visiting the fields. She also influenced his ministry of words: he never published his own writing until she first read and approved it, and she gauged his sermon when he preached and signaled if it should end. On one occasion, he ended his sermon prematurely when she coughed accidentally.

Maud Chapman grew ill in California in 1940. After she improved, the

Chapmans proceeded to their next appointments in Oklahoma, but she developed pneumonia and died in Oklahoma City on February 14. She was buried in Bethany.

J. B. Chapman wrote a few days later: "My wife always wanted a home. [Each time] we thought we were settled . . . God, in His providence, stirred up our nest . . . [This] was always a sacrifice to her, and in delirium during her last sickness, she would still murmur, "I want a home." Thank God, she has found it now, even though it was her lot to be a pilgrim and a stranger upon this earth." His book, *My Wife*, was a vehicle for his grief and a tribute to her life and their marriage.

Louise R. Chapman

**Louise Robinson**

Two years after his first wife died, J. B. Chapman married Louise Robinson. Chapman's wives shared a common piety and deep love for the church, but their lives differed significantly. Maud, married 37 years, died relatively young. Louise lived to 100, but was single for all but five years of her life. In hindsight, it is clear that she was an independent woman most of her life, and that the church was her real family.

Louise Robinson was born October 9, 1892 in a log cabin near La Center, Washington. Her family was unchurched, but she was converted in her senior year of high school in a country Baptist church. She taught school for four years. She united with the Nazarenes and perceived a clear call to preach in 1915.

She entered Northwest Nazarene College the next year, where she was befriended and influenced by president H. Orton Wiley and dean Olive Winchester. She struggled to claim the grace of entire sanctification, but was unable until she accepted God's call to be a missionary in Africa. She graduated with honors in June 1920, was ordained to the ministry that summer by R. T. Williams, and left for Africa in October. Audrey Williamson has noted that Louise Robinson's career can be understood only from the standpoint of one who took, with utmost seriousness, the ordination charge: "Take thou authority."

Louise was stationed at Sabie, Transvaal, for four years. In 1924, she went to Endzingeni, Swaziland to superintend the Girls' Training School. There, she eventually cared for hundreds of young women. Some of her students became evangelists and Bible teachers, others preachers' spouses. She instructed them in English and Zulu, led their Bible studies, and taught practical skills. When the buildings were no longer sufficient, she constructed new ones. By 1930, she was helping train preachers at the Men's Training School. She pastored the local church at different periods and, for many years, supervised about 15 outstations in the area. Evangelism was her favorite task. "Africa is all I see," she wrote, "and her people are, to me, the most beautiful of all the tribes of earth."

Louise Robinson Chapman preaching

Louise Robinson returned to the United States on furlough in 1940. World war delayed her return to Africa. She married J. B. Chapman on June 20, 1942, ending her missionary career. She was nearly 50.

She brought to her marriage a convivial personality and shared with Chapman the storyteller's art, passion for evangelism, and a common experience in the preaching life. She traveled with him constantly and spoke on missions at assemblies where he presided. She was with him when he died at their home at Indian Lake in Michigan in July 1947. For her, the marriage was all too brief.

Williamsons and Chapmans

In 1948, she was elected president of the Nazarene Foreign Missionary Society. Every bit of Louise Chapman's preaching skills and missionary experience were poured into that job in the next 16 years as she planned, organized, promoted, and spoke. NFMS membership tripled during her tenure, rising to over 225,000. She visited the fields, built the Alabaster program, and, throughout her presidency, served on the General Board. Her writings included *Africa, O, Africa* (1945), partly autobiographical; *The Problem of Africa* (1952); and *Footprints in Africa* (1959).

Her advocacy of missions continued in retirement. She continued visiting mission areas until her health no longer permitted. At Casa Robles, the missionary retirement center where she settled, she was united with friends of many years standing. Her mind was filled with cherished memories, her years with J. B. Chapman among the dearest. She died at 100 on April 12, 1993.

J. B. and Louise Robinson Chapman

# The Relevance of Our Story

An Endnote by the Author

Martin Marty is a perceptive analyst of America's religious past and present. In 1991, he gave the keynote address at the annual meeting of the Association of Nazarene Sociologists of Religion. Afterward, he simply listened for a day and a half as Nazarenes spoke to one another. In the final session, host Bill Sullivan asked for his observations. Marty had detected anxiety among Nazarenes over a perceived loss of denominational identity. He also noted the fascination of some with the Willow Creek Church model. He noted that the Willow Creek church was in the vicinity of Chicago, his home. His advice: if Nazarenes imitate the Willow Creek model, they should become disciples of Willow Creek theology. Theological assumptions always underlie a particular way of "doing church." However, he warned, this will just facilitate a sense of drift. It would be far better, he said, to study our founders, understand their intentions, sift their vision, and ask how this can inform present and future ministry. These were wise words, spoken by a true Lutheran immersed in his own tradition.

I once attended a conference in which a speaker noted that people who do not know their own history are compelled to invent one, since we must have a past as a frame of reference. In recent years, various writers have sought to make our history accessible to Nazarenes. Carl Bangs presented a fresh look at *Phineas F. Bresee: His Life in Methodism, the Holiness Movement, and the Church of the Nazarene* (1995). He did so in the anticipation that Nazarenes might rediscover their most revered founder.

Now a new denominational history has appeared. *Our Watchword and Song: The Centennial History of the Church of the Nazarene* (2009) is a comprehensive story of the Nazarenes that begins with the Wesleyan revival and continues to the 21st century. It presents the story of a denomination with British theological roots that took shape in America and developed into an international church in which Nazarenes outside the United States now make up 65 percent of the church membership. I urge you to read it.

I frequently read journals of missiology. Missiology is a theological discipline in which the study of missions history continually loops back to inform mission theory and practice. The Nazarene Roots Project is conceived in the same spirit—to make accessible a usable past. Pietism, early Methodism, the Free Methodists, the Wesleyan Methodists, the Wesleyan-Holiness Movement, the Church of the Nazarene—each originated as a fresh project of Christian renewal and reform. We should know these stories, since reformation is the church's continuing imperative, as H. Richard Niebuhr famously said. For that reason and others, the stories in this book are truly part of our own.